ALMOST AN ORPHAN

ALMOST AN ORPHAN
A Memoir

Lawrence H. Cohen

HANNACROIX CREEK BOOKS, INC.
Stamford, Connecticut

Published by:

HANNACROIX CREEK BOOKS, INC.
1127 High Ridge Road, #110
Stamford, CT 06905-1203 USA

www.hannacroixcreekbooks.com
e-mail: hannacroix@aol.com

Follow us on twitter: http://www.twitter.com/hannacroixcreek

(Trade Paperback)
ISBN: 13-digit: 978-1-889262-98-7
10-digit: 1-889262-98-6

Cover design by Jan Yager
Front cover montage of contributed photos covering the author's life from ages four through ten: Front of the apartment house in Manhattan where the author lived with his Grandma Fannie and Aunt Lilly from the ages of 7 to 10.
Author at the age of four.
Pictures throughout the book of the author
and his wife are contributed photos

Interior Layout & Design by Scribe Freelance | www.scribefreelance.com

Library of Congress Cataloging-in-Publication Data

Cohen, Lawrence H., 1923-
Almost an orphan / Lawrence H. Cohen.
p. cm.
ISBN 978-1-889262-98-7 (trade pbk.)
1. Cohen, Lawrence H., 1923- 2. Teachers--New York (State)--New York--
Biography. 3. Little Neck (New York, N.Y.)--Biography. I. Title.
CT275.C6669A3 2011
371.10092--dc22
[B]
2010024024

Prologue

IN MY HIGH SCHOOL FRENCH class, presided over by a middle-aged gentleman named Monsieur Perry, we read a text called *Le Petit Chose* by Alphonse Daudet. Literally translated, the title in English would have been *The Little Thing*, but this didn't quite capture the real meaning which in everyday language would have been "The Little What's-It's-Name" or "The Little Nobody."

While I do not remember the entire plot of the story, I do know it was about a French waif who was sent from one family to another. Sometimes he was treated well and sometimes poorly by the adults in his life. But until the end when he became a "somebody," he was denied his personhood because of circumstances beyond his control.

As I continued on through high school and into adulthood, that story always appealed to me for some unknown reason. It wasn't until years later that I figured out why. In many ways, *Le Petit Chose* lived a life similar to mine when I was a child. I didn't grow up in a traditional family with a mother, father and siblings although my life started out that way. Like *Le Petit Chose,* I was sent hither and yon to various caretakers—all of whom were decent and kind to me—but none of them could counteract my perception of myself as a "nobody." For as a child, I was missing one of the basics necessities of life: a loving family.

There is another reason why I recall that particular high school French class so vividly. Seated in front of me was a bright young girl with brown eyes and brown hair braided into strands. Whenever Monsieur Perry asked a question about the history of France or a translation of a French word, her hand shot up like a "jack in the box" and invariably she was right. To Monsieur Perry that bright young girl was "Mademoiselle Grossman." To me she was "Celia," who later became my wife and helped me become a "somebody" who was loved as part of a stable family.

I suppose you could say that is the silver lining in my story because once I learned to appreciate and value the concept of family, and once it was in my grasp, I never let it go. What follows is my journey through life from a "nobody" to a "somebody."

CHAPTER ONE
Earliest memories

MY BIRTH CERTIFICATE SAYS THAT I was born in a hospital in Uniontown, Pennsylvania on October 10, 1923 at 9:01 a.m. My parents were Herman Cohen, a 27-year-old store manager from New York, and Dora Brown, a 26-year-old housewife from Cleveland, Ohio.

My father was a handsome man with a healthy build, neither fat nor thin. He had dark brown curly hair and brown eyes. My mother had a thin build and green eyes. She spent most of her adult years in a state hospital in Cleveland.

My memories about my earliest years are vague, partly because they happened so long ago, and partly because my parents did not believe in explaining why certain events were going on in our lives, such as the illness of my mother and the break-up of our family.

However, a few memories remain. I remember sitting at a table coloring with my older sister Joan. My mother looked at my coloring book and remarked that I should have kept my colors within the lines of the drawing. Joan's coloring was neat; her crayons did not stray beyond the borders of the picture she was coloring.

One day my mother promised to take me shopping with her. I looked forward to the outing, but for some reason my mother changed her mind. Instead of going shopping with her, I was sent to school with my sister Joan, a kind of informal babysitting arrangement which the school had agreed to. I sat in the back of the classroom and watched the proceedings through the eyes of a four-year-old.

While I was sitting next to my sister, I suddenly remembered that I had been promised a shopping trip with my mother and somehow the plans were switched. Not only had plans been changed, but no one had told me about it. I started to cry, upsetting the whole classroom. The teacher tried to find the reason for my distress, but I was unable to express the cause for my loud bawling. The crisis ended when my sister was told to take me home.

I remember a Fourth of July fireworks display that my father had planned just for our family. A week before the holiday, my father started to amass a large assortment of fireworks, rockets, firecrackers and sparklers, which he stored on top of our icebox in the kitchen. My father warned me not to touch any of the paraphernalia, and for once I obeyed.

On that Fourth of July, just as it was turning dark, my father set off the rockets, using our front lawn as our launching pad. Joan and I "o-o-h d" and "a-a-h d" as we heard the swish of the rockets racing skyward, and we thrilled to the bursts of colors in the darkening sky. We each received some sparklers which we could hold in our hands. When lit with a match, the sparklers emitted bright, star-like sparks that were harmless but fun to watch.

One spring day a gray-haired black man came to our backyard. He dug a garden for planting flowers and vegetables. He made neat rows in the dark brown soil and then he planted lettuce, tomatoes and other vegetables. No one told me about the garden, but I now believe it was meant as therapy for my mother who might have been suffering from post-partum depression, a mental condition not yet recognized in those days, following the birth of my younger sister, Esther Ruth.

Our neighbor was a kind lady whose name I can't remember. One day she gave me a bean to plant in our garden and told me to watch it grow. The plant grew tall and started to flower. No one told me to wait until the plant bore fruit so I cut off the flower and proudly presented it to our neighbor. She tried to hide her disappointment as she told me I had cut the plant too soon but she thanked me for the flower anyway.

I remember a time before we moved to New York when my father was working as the manager in the shoe department of a large store. My father had the idea he could care of me by taking me to work with him. (You could say he implemented the "Take a Child to Work" program a few years early.)

My father had no idea what a five-year-old boy would do for a whole working day in a department store. Fortunately the problem was solved when a kindly black elevator operator named Sam agreed to watch over me. Sam taught me how to operate the elevator. This was in the days before pushbutton elevators. It was a fairly complicated process. For a boy of my age, operating an elevator was an enormous thrill and, thankfully, Sam was a patient man who showed me how to move the lever on the control assembly. You had to move the lever to the left to go down and then return the lever to the middle position to stop the elevator.

It was quite understandable that at first my handling of the elevator control was a little jerky. I would stop too suddenly and the elevator would bounce slightly, or I would stop it when it was not quite flush with the landing, either above or below it. Sam, the professional operator, would stand behind me and tolerantly correct my mistakes.

I soon learned that the trick to a smooth operation of the elevator was to stop it slightly before reaching the floor landing and let the elevator car glide easily until it was perfectly level with the adjacent floor. Under Sam's guidance I soon learned how to bring the elevator to a smooth landing. I delighted in my accomplishment and wished I could have this job for the rest of my life.

However, my career as an elevator operator was soon terminated. It seemed that my father's solution of keeping me occupied in the department store while he held down the job of manager of the shoe department could not last.

Evidently my father thought it would be impossible for him to work and take care of three children at the same time, so he sought the help of his family, who decided that no one of them could assume the task of raising three children in addition to their own children.

Therefore, we three children, Joan, Esther Ruth, and I, were to be separated. My older sister, Joan, was placed with my father's sister, Aunt Mamie, and her husband, Uncle Harold, in New York. Unfortunately, Joan died of a severe case of pneumonia soon after moving in with Aunt Mamie.

My younger sister, Esther Ruth, was sent to live in Pittsburgh with another of my father's sisters, Aunt Dora, and her husband, Uncle Ben, and their grown children, Janet, Bob and Philip. (Esther Ruth is still alive today, and is living in California.)

Now it would be my turn.

CHAPTER TWO

My father and I take a train ride to New York

ONE DAY MY FATHER WOKE ME UP early in the morning, helped me get dressed and packed some of my clothes into a tiny valise. I was about to take my first train ride from Connellsville to New York on the Baltimore and Ohio railroad. My Father didn't explain why we were going on a train ride or what we would do in New York. I was just thrilled to be going on a train and I didn't ask many questions.

I don't remember much about the train ride, but I do remember reaching the Bronx apartment of my grandparents, Fannie and Barney Cohen. They were having breakfast in the kitchen at a table covered with a shiny blue oilcloth when we arrived. Grandpa invited me to sit down next to him and offered me some coffee. It wasn't exactly coffee; it was really milk flavored with a teaspoonful of coffee, but it tasted good to me.

In the days that followed, I became aware that my family life had changed. My father went back to his job in Connellsville, Pennsylvania, and I became the ward of my grandmother, grandfather and Aunt Lillie, who lived with them.

Once again, I was not told why this break-up of my nuclear family took place. Unlike the model families we would see later portrayed on television, where the adults always explained what was going on to their children, my family believed in back-room diplomacy where children were protected by not being informed.

"What you don't know won't hurt you," was the family motto. It would be many years later before I could infer what had actually happened to my family.

As I alluded to earlier, when I was four and my sister Joan was seven, my mother gave birth to her third child, Esther Ruth.

Apparently this birth brought on my mother's post-partum depression, which eventually landed her in a state hospital in Cleveland, Ohio. There she was frequently visited by her sister, my Aunt Ray. Although my mother's condition improved somewhat, she remained in the hospital for the rest of her life.

Early years in my grandparents' home

IT DIDN'T TAKE LONG FOR MY new surrogate parents to realize I was old enough to be in school. This problem became the province of my grandfather, a religious man who thought that I should have a Hebrew education in a *Yeshiva*.

One morning, after I was dressed and breakfasted, my grandfather took me by the hand and brought me to the first grade of a *Yeshiva* on Washington Avenue in the Bronx. I was brought to the classroom of a gentle lady, who was to be my first teacher. She apparently realized how frightened I must have been.

Part of my bewilderment of all this was due to the fact that no one had prepared me for this event. My grandfather soon left me in the care of this sympathetic teacher who tried her best to make me feel welcome into my new life as a *Yeshiva* pupil. However, I had no understanding of what was happening to me. I had entered first grade in the middle of the term. All of the other boys knew the routines, but all this was strange to me. What was I doing in this strange place? Where would I eat lunch? How would I get back home? Did these adults even know where I lived?

Somehow I got through the morning. At noon I was taken to the huge lunchroom in the basement of the *Yeshiva* where a series of long tables covered in oilcloth and seating about ten children each were arrayed across the room. From both sides of the tables boys sat talking to one another in loud voices waiting for the food to be served. The smell of some kind of fish, not my favorite food, permeated the room. When the food arrived, the boys attacked it gleefully as they continued their loud conversations. I avoided the fish dish and contented myself with a small container of milk, which I sipped through a straw. The room had that telltale "fishy" smell, which lingered long after the meal was served. Even though my grandfather paid for my lunch, I never stepped foot inside the cafeteria again. Instead I went out to the yard to play until the bell summoned us back to class for the afternoon session, which turned out to be my Hebrew class.

The curriculum for the *Yeshiva* was divided into two parts: English and Hebrew. We were taught in English in the mornings; then we had lunch in the basement cafeteria, and after lunch we were taught in Hebrew. Our English instruction consisted of reading, writing, arithmetic, history, geography and music. The music was taught in an assembly where one teacher played the piano and we sang songs.

I remember a rousing pep rally song that was a paraphrase of the college fight songs popular in those days. It went like this:

Stand up and cheer. Stand up for our Yeshiva,
For today we raise the blue and white,
Above the rest. Above the rest.

Our boys are fighting
And we're about to win the fray.
We've got the team. We've got the steam.
And this is our Yeshiva's day!

We sang the song lustily even though we didn't have any team to put on the field.

On Fridays we only had a half-day of Hebrew so that we could get ready for our Sabbath holiday at sundown. To make up for the missed English class, we had to come in for a half-day on Sunday morning.

I don't remember much about the teaching in English except that we learned to read from a basal reader called *Dicky Dare*. It was very similar to the basal readers used in public schools at that time. The famous *Dick and Jane* series was probably in fashion then. I also remember that phonics played a large part in the reading program.

One particular incident comes to mind as we were learning the "IG" family. The teacher wrote the word "big" on the blackboard and we all called out the word "big." Then she wrote the word "dig," and we all called out the word "dig." Then she wrote the word "pig" and for some reason we all broke up in laughter at that word. Somehow by learning all the word families and by following the adventures of *Dicky Dare*, we learned to read.

Our school's backyard was a simple affair of packed dirt. There was no playground equipment of any kind, but we didn't miss it much. We could use the dirt surface to make small holes in the ground for our marble games. If a player knocked a marble into the hole with his marble he got to keep his opponent's marble.

This backyard playground was also used at the end of the school day as we waited for our school bus to take us back home. Our bus was called the "Second Trip Bus" because the *Yeshiva* hired only one bus for all its students. The bus driver, therefore, had to make two trips to take of all the students, so some students had to wait until the bus returned from its first trip. As "Second Trip Bus" students, we didn't mind waiting because it gave us a chance to play punch ball in our dilapidated yard.

The punch ball games were organized by the older boys. Since I was one of the younger players, I was assigned to play the outfield where I could do the least damage to my team. One day, however, one of the older boys punched the pink ball far into the outfield in my direction. I didn't have to run much to get to the fly ball because it was headed right at me. The ball landed right in my outstretched hands, and I managed to hold onto it. I had saved my team from a certain home run by our opponents, and I was hailed as the hero of the day. Then someone shouted, "The 'Second Trip Bus' is here!" This announcement meant the end of our game as we all dispersed to the front of the *Yeshiva* where our bus was waiting to take us home.

In the afternoons, after lunch, the younger students' curriculum centered on learning to speak, read and write in Hebrew. It is amazing how quickly young minds can absorb a foreign language. Within a year I was speaking Hebrew fluently and could also read and write quite well in that language. However, because I never used those skills once I left the *Yeshiva*, I can neither speak nor understand Hebrew today. I still retain some reading ability, but it is nowhere near the skill I once had at the *Yeshiva*.

Hebrew is one of those foreign languages that should be taught at an earlier age than it is presently taught in the United States because younger minds are more capable of learning languages. The other point is that foreign languages have to be used in order to be maintained.

There are some lessons to be drawn from my experience in learning. As I grew older the Hebrew classes became more difficult, emphasizing grammar and reading from the five books of Moses.

Teaching the older boys was left to the male teachers, some of whom were decent human beings and teachers, and some who were not meant to be teachers. I remember one class in which we had to conjugate verbs in Hebrew. The teacher just gave out assignments to conjugate verbs, but he didn't bother to teach us how to handle the conjugation or what pattern to use. Those students who mastered the task were patted on the head, and those who didn't were smacked on the palms of the hands with a ruler. Perhaps this form of corporal punishment played a hand in my later decision to leave the *Yeshiva* in favor of the public schools.

Most of the teachers, however, taught us well, and I made good progress in my studies. One day while I was in Hebrew class, my grandfather walked into the classroom. He was greeted politely by the teacher, as though this visit had been expected, and asked to sit down and observe the lesson in progress. The teacher then called upon me to read in Hebrew, translate into English and answer questions which were asked in Hebrew. I performed flawlessly, and Grandpa Barney seemed pleased as he left the classroom. At the end of the day, Grandpa reappeared to take me home by trolley car instead of letting me go home the usual way by bus.

As we left the building we saw a food cart, which was common in those days. It was mounted on four wheels and had all kinds of delicious food for sale. There were hot sweet potatoes, hot chick peas, dried prunes and apricots, dried apple slices and coconut slices. My grandfather approached the cart and told me to buy anything I wanted. It was his way of telling me how proud he was of my progress in Hebrew.

CHAPTER THREE

The death of grandpa Barney

GRANDPA BARNEY WAS SMALL IN stature with a rotund body frame. The top of his head was bald and was framed by silvery hair around the back and sides. He was a quiet man who seldom raised his voice, but most of all he was a religious man.

Not far from our ground-floor apartment at 1479 Jessup Avenue in the Bronx was a storefront place of worship called a shul. This is where Grandpa went to pray on Friday evenings, Saturday mornings and Saturday nights. There were many storefront shuls in the Bronx. They had once been small stores consisting of one room for keeping stock and one room for selling some kind of merchandise. When these stores went out of business or when the proprietors moved away, these storefronts were bought or rented by Jewish communities that needed a place to worship. Eventually the congregation hoped to save enough money to build a synagogue or temple.

There was no question that I would attend services with my grandfather on Friday nights and Saturday mornings, but on Saturday evenings Grandpa excused me from attending services and went alone.

At the end of the Saturday night service, the congregation arranged a little collation consisting of pickled herring, whitefish, schnapps, and beer. One Saturday evening while my grandfather was in shul, the phone rang in our apartment. My father, who was now living with us, answered. "Hello."

"Is this the Cohen family?" asked an excited voice. Without waiting for an answer, the voice continued, "Come to the shul right away. Something has happened to your father."

My Dad and I rushed to the shul where we found Grandpa lying on his back on a table. His tie had been removed as well as the detachable collar which he usually wore. His face was flushed and his breathing was labored. The congregation surrounded the table with worried looks on their faces. That was the last I saw of my grandfather for he was rushed to the hospital and died soon after. We learned later that the cause of death was a heart attack caused by a blood clot. The family was devastated by grandpa's death.

Grandma Fannie could not overcome her grief for a long time. Grandpa had been the center of this family and without him the family seemed to have broken apart. Later we learned that Grandpa had contributed a great deal of money for a new synagogue, which was eventually completed soon after his death.

Grandpa was from the town of Vilna in Poland where he met Fannie, married her and brought her to the state of Pennsylvania in the United States. The couple had very little money, but Grandpa managed to eke out a living as a peddler buying goods and selling them to farmers scattered throughout Pennsylvania. The farms in those days were rather isolated, not near the stores which were in towns. The farmers and their wives were happy to see Grandpa's horse-drawn wagon with its wares. They bought linens and towels and aprons and tools. Then they told Grandpa what they needed for his next visit, so Grandpa made enough money to raise his large family, including his wife and eleven children.

Eventually Grandpa saved enough money to buy some houses and to become a landlord. In time he amassed enough money to abandon his peddling business and live off the income from his properties.

One of my fondest memories of my grandfather was how he used to tell me stories from the Bible on Saturday afternoons after the noonday meal. He would sit with me at the cleared kitchen table with the Bible in his hand. He would read a few sentences from the Hebrew text and slowly translate the story from Hebrew into English for me. This was his way of fulfilling his religious obligation to teach the concepts of the Jewish religion to his children, but more importantly to me, it was Grandpa's way of showing that he loved me.

CHAPTER FOUR

Moving from the Bronx to Manhattan

SOON AFTER GRANDPA'S DEATH we moved from the Bronx to the Fort Washington section of Manhattan. Our new address became 44 Bennett Avenue. Of course I didn't want to leave my familiar neighborhood of Jessup Avenue because all my friends were there and the streets were fairly familiar to me.

I would miss the schoolyard on Shakespeare Avenue where we climbed the fence to play handball on weekends. And near the storefront *shul* was the candy store where I exchanged my pennies for licorice sticks or button candy. Down the hill from our apartment building was the famous Featherbed Lane along which, according to legend, George Washington's army had been trying to escape from New York. To help muffle the sound of the horses' footsteps, the citizens laid down their feather mattresses on the streets, helping the army to escape unnoticed by the British.

Featherbed Lane was the neighborhood's primary shopping area. I was often sent to the market there to buy "loose milk" for ten cents a dipper. I carried a quart-sized aluminum pail with a tight-fitting lid which I handed to the dairyman. He filled my pail with a dipper full of milk taken from a ten-gallon pail. This was before the Board of Health banned "loose milk" because it was unsanitary.

On Featherbed Lane one could also find an ice cream parlor with whirling ceiling fans, wire-backed chairs, marble tables and of course, delicious ice cream. Was there any other neighborhood that could match all that?

As it turned out, I came to learn that Bennett Avenue possessed a charm all its own. It was a tiny street one block west of Broadway and 180th Street in Manhattan. It was twelve blocks long running from 180th Street to 192nd Street.

One of the best features of Bennett Avenue, as far as we

children were concerned, was its gentle slope going from south to north from 180ᵗʰ Street all the way down to 191ˢᵗ Street. This made for great sleigh riding in winter when the snow fell and the cold weather turned the snow into shiny ice, especially around the iron manhole covers located in the middle of each block.

The few cars that used Bennett Avenue during snowy weather did a good job of packing down the snow-covered street. When the weather obliged by turning cold and staying cold for almost a week, Bennett Avenue would then become a version of a bobsled run. In those days of the early 1930's the Sanitation Department didn't plow the side streets after a large snow fall, and the tall buildings on either side of the street kept the sun from melting our sleigh ride course. We kids could sleigh ride down the hill for five or six days at a time.

The fact that I never owned a sled didn't deter me from enjoying sleigh riding season. The neighborhood was packed with kids who did own sleds and they were happy to share them with me because the extra weight of two on a sled meant a faster ride. My friend would lie prone on his Flexible Flyer with his hands on the steering rod at the top of the sled. I would stand behind and when given the "ready" signal I would give the sled a running push and then jump on the sled on top of my friend.

He would steer the fast moving sled toward the middle of the street where the icy manhole covers were located. We would aim for the edge of the manhole cover because that was where the ice had accumulated. When we hit the edge of the manhole cover, the fast-moving sled would accelerate our speed. Then we would steer toward the next ice-caked manhole cover and the sled would gain even more speed. Since there were some two or three manhole covers to each block, the sled would be going at a wind-whistling speed by the time we reached the end of our ride at 191ˢᵗ Street, where someone had placed some ashes to stop our swift ride.

At the end of the ride, we would pull our sleds back up the hill walking on either side of the road and leaving the center for the other down-hill riders who were hurtling down the street. Once we were back up the hill, my friend and I would switch places; I would be on the bottom steering the sled, and he would be the pusher and ride on top of me.

After school we would spend hours on the icy slopes of Bennett Avenue. When it turned dark, we reluctantly went home for supper. Sometimes on the weekends we even got to ride at night. During the winter season on Bennett Avenue God must have received many conflicting messages. Grown-ups who had to go to work prayed for dry, warm weather. Children, on the other hand, prayed for snow and freezing cold. Maybe God in His wisdom satisfied both factions by producing a little of both.

In addition to the fortuitous hill which made for excellent sleigh riding, Bennett Avenue had another treasure: an empty lot.

My friends and I had no idea who owned the empty lot, and as far as we were concerned the plot of unused land belonged to us. It was our playground. Years later, the large piece of land became another apartment building. But in the 1930's when I was ten years old, that empty lot was our football field in winter, our baseball field in summer, and our campground all year round where we would dig holes in the ground, build a small fire over the holes, and roast potatoes until they were black on the outside but delicious on the inside.

During the winter the older boys would play a form of football, which was called "Association." I think the derivation of the name comes from Ireland where football teams were sponsored by groups of businesses called "Associations." The game involved moving the football over a goal line by either running or passing; no blocking or tackling was involved in this tamer form of football. I used to watch the older boys play, standing on the sidelines. One day an odd number of boys showed up for a game, and since one team was short a player, a boy named Stan approached me.

"Hey, kid. You want to play?" he asked. "Sure!" I answered and ran to take my place on Stan's team.

Stan was even older than the other boys. He must have been in high school, so he was automatically captain of his team. I was the youngest member of the group, but I had watched many games, so I knew how the game was played. Aside from knowing the game, I was a fast runner and knew how to get free of the player who was covering me, trying to prevent me from catching the ball. When Stan saw that I was out in the open, he threw the ball high in the air in what is called a leading pass. The ball was high in front of me so that I had to run to catch up to it and grab it in my two hands. When I caught the ball, I was near the goal line and scored six points for my team.

The other team players were surprised that a little kid could catch passes so well, and after the first goal they paid more attention to me and tried to cover me better. However, Stan was an excellent passer and kept throwing me leading passes, most of which I managed to catch. After that first game, I became a member of the football gang and had no trouble getting picked to play on a team.

Aside from our empty lot which we used as a playground, our neighborhood had another important asset: the RKO movie theater, located on Broadway and 180th Street. No matter what was on the bill, we flocked to the movie theater on Saturday afternoons where we were treated to a cartoon, a review of the news (Fox Movietone News), an adventure chapter like *The Perils of Pauline,* and the feature film. Sometimes, they had a sing-a-long where the words of popular songs were flashed on the screen and a bouncing ping-pong ball was used to keep the time.

While most of my friends attended the shows regularly on Saturdays, no matter what was playing, a few of the older boys and I had a special connection to the RKO Theater: we were known as the "Newsette Boys." In those days the RKO theaters used to send a one-sheet flyer, folded into four pages, to announce the coming attractions and to present a little gossip about the film stars. The flyer was called a "Newsette," and people could have it mailed to them free of charge by filling out a form with their names and addresses. A secretary would take the forms and make a master list of people who would receive the "Newsette" by mail. Then she would make addressed envelopes for all the names on the list. Now, someone had to fold the flyers, insert them into the addressed envelopes, and seal the envelopes. That process became the task of the "Newsette Boys."

We worked at this job once a week for several hours each time until the task was completed and received minimal wages for our labors. However, a valuable perk came with the job: the "Newsette Boys" received free admission to the show each week. We would just approach the ticket taker at the entrance to the theater and say, "Newsette Boy," and in we would go. I can't recall how long this job lasted or why it terminated. Perhaps the Department of Labor got involved and asked if child-labor laws were being ignored because the work was being done by minors under the age of sixteen. Nonetheless, I saw a great many shows during my short career as a "Newsette Boy."

Another interesting development concerning the RKO Theater was the attempt to revive Vaudeville, a series of acts by comedians, acrobats, mimes, singers and magicians, accompanied by a live orchestra which played in the pit of the large theater. The closest thing to Vaudeville which was popular in the twenties was the *Ed Sullivan Show* in the sixties and seventies. Ed Sullivan, the show's host, was able to present all kinds of artists like those just mentioned. This was as close to old fashioned Vaudeville as one can get.

Before the movie began, the lights would dim and the spotlights would beam on a large orchestra which would begin playing. When the orchestra finished its number, two large signs on either side of the stage would light up with the name of the first act. If it was an acrobatic act, the sign might read, "The Flying Wallendas." The orchestra would then play an introductory theme as the acrobats took center stage.

During their performance, the orchestra would play appropriate accompaniment, like "Over the Waves" or a drum roll to highlight a particularly difficult acrobatic feat. At the end of the act, the orchestra would play a rousing departing theme, and the signs would announce the next act. There were usually five or six acts to each show which would last for one week.

When the movie feature changed, a new Vaudeville show would come to the RKO 180th Street Theater. I remember one act in particular where a man dressed in a clown's outfit would come on stage bringing a large easel with large sheets of blank white paper. Without saying a word, the clown would take a black crayon and draw a huge picture of an object like a water pump. Then the clown would attach a real handle to the easel, pump the handle, and real water would come out into a cup which the clown had removed from his baggy pants. The clown drank the water as the audience laughed and clapped.

I loved to watch Vaudeville and went to see the same show three or four times a week. I could do this because as a "Newsette Boy" I had a free pass to all the shows. After almost a year, the attempt to revive Vaudeville ended in failure. The audiences became too small to warrant the expenses needed to present the shows. A fitting epitaph for the experiment with Vaudeville would be "It was great while it lasted."

CHAPTER FIVE

P.S. 132, Manhattan

NEEDLESS TO SAY, A ten-year-old boy doesn't spend all his time in empty lots and theaters because schooling plays such an important role in children's lives. Once again I was enrolled in a public school in the middle of the term. My father brought me to P.S. 132 Manhattan at 185 Wadsworth Avenue. My new teacher was Mrs. Wallach, who greeted my arrival with a remark that previously was said by Goldilocks: "My, what big ears you have. You must have excellent hearing."

Mrs. Wallach was right about the first sentence because my ears did form a large part of my face, but she was wrong about my hearing ability. It was no better or worse than the average child's. However, Mrs. Wallach proved to be an excellent, caring teacher, who helped me make a smooth transition from the *Yeshiva* in the Bronx to a public school. She was a matronly woman with dark brown curly hair with hints of gray. She wore wire-rimmed glasses, and her face wore a calm expression.

This kind teacher was a great believer in the reward system. In her desk drawer along with pens, pencils and paper clips she kept a box of Schraft's chocolates, which she dispensed frequently to deserving boys and girls. Children who got 100 on their spelling or math tests were invited to line up near her desk and select one piece of the delicious chocolate candy.

Not only was academic performance rewarded, but bravery also counted. There came a time when the school nurse had to inoculate all the children against the flu or some other disease. Each child in Mrs. Wallach's class received a piece of chocolate to ease the pain which accompanied the shot. When the candy from one box was depleted, another box appeared.

On Fridays we were allowed to do our penmanship papers and

our spelling papers in pen and ink. This took place well before the invention of the ball point pen. Instead we used a wooden pen holder with a curved notch at one end to hold a steel-pen point. The ink supply came from small glass ink wells which were inserted into the holes in our desks and were located in the upper right-hand corner. The ink wells were filled early on Friday morning by the ink monitor, a child with demonstrated skills in handling a large bottle of ink with a keen eye and a steady hand. To be sure, using ink with those crude instruments had its risks. Too much ink would cause a blot on the hoped-for neat paper.

The antidote for the blot was a blotter, a small piece of cardboard with absorbent tissue-like paper on one side. Placing the blotter over the ink blot would dry up the wet ink, but it could not remove the stain all together. Another risk was in pressing too hard on the pen. This would cause the pen point to splatter over the paper in little droplets of ink. Sometimes the splatter would go as far as the shirt or blouse of the person sitting in front, causing all kinds of grumbling. That is why Mrs. Wallach wisely confined the use of ink to one day a week.

Aside from rewarding her pupils with chocolate and teaching them the skill necessary to write with ink, Mrs. Wallach was an avid teacher of rote songs. Even seventy years later some of those ditties, both words and music, are rattling round in my head. One was called *The Postman*:

> *Postman, postman, why is he late again?*
> *Postman, postman, where can he be?*
> *Here he comes hurrying,*
> *Here he comes scurrying,*
> *Listen, listen, yes it is he.*

Along with music, Mrs. Wallach was fond of poetry, which she taught with enthusiasm. So it came to pass that our grade held a poetry recitation contest. Mrs. Wallach chose me to represent our class in the contest with a poem called "Try, Try Again" by W.E. Hickson (1803-1870). The first few lines go like this:

'Tis a lesson you should heed, try, try again.
If at first you don't succeed, Try, try again.

The poem went along in the same vein in which the second line of the verse was always, "Try, try again." So I dutifully memorized the whole poem and felt confident that I could pull it off. When my turn came to recite before the fourth and fifth grade assembly, I spoke loud and clear with emphasis and expression. I was going along beautifully, a cinch to win a prize until I got to the last line. I had failed to notice that the poet had tired of using the line, "Try, try, again" and therefore switched his last line to read "Try and try again. Since I had omitted the "and" I was disqualified, and the child who had recited with no expression whatsoever, but who got all the words right, won first prize.

Disheartened, I returned to our classroom in disgrace. Even kind Mrs. Wallach offered me no solace. Her expression told me that I had let her down, and the drawer with the box of chocolates remained closed.

Eventually the ignominy of leaving out an "and" in "Try, Try, Again" was forgotten and I was promoted to the fifth grade where I performed magnificently as King Ferdinand of Spain, who was against giving any money to the crazy Columbus fellow who thought the world was round. My wife, Queen Isabella, was played by a pretty brunette named Harriet. As Isabella, she convinced me, Ferdinand, to give this Italian enough money to buy three ships, but I made sure that the ships were small.

While the play took place on a tiny stage in front of eight classes, there was no real auditorium in P.S. 132, Manhattan. Instead there were eight classrooms, four on each side of a long hallway. Each classroom was enclosed by a series of sliding doors on tracks. When it was time for an assembly, some monitors opened up all of the classrooms by sliding the doors to the back and sides of the hall. In other words, the classrooms with their doors pushed back became the auditorium. When the assembly program was over, the monitors returned the doors to their places and the ten separate classrooms became self-contained classes again.

No one ever explained why the school had no real auditorium, but my guess is that during the 1920's and thirties, the Board of Education was trying to save money in building new schools. An auditorium took up a lot of space, required many seats, a stage with curtains, a screen and lights. It had to be heated in the fall, winter, and part of the spring. All of this expense was for an auditorium, which was vacant for a good part of each day. So the school architects planned this arrangement of movable walls as a substitute for a regular auditorium.

I wished I could have stayed at P.S. 132 until the eighth grade, for it was a good, friendly place in which to learn. But this was not to be because changes were occurring in the family and they were getting ready to move once again.

CHAPTER SIX

My summer visits

AS A TEN-YEAR-OLD, I was shunted around as my surrogate parents tried to ease the burden on Grandma and Aunt Lillie by sending me to live with various aunts and uncles during the summer months when school was out. However, I did not resent these moves because my aunts in Pittsburgh and Fairmont, West Virginia welcomed me into their spacious houses.

My first summer visits were to my Aunt Dora's house in Pittsburgh. For my first trip, my father brought me to Penn Station, bought my ticket on the Baltimore and Ohio, the old B&O Railroad, and saw me onto the train. The trains in those days had coal-fired steam engines. They were noisy and sooty trains, but I loved watching the passing scenery from my window seat.

The ride lasted eight or more hours, but I didn't mind. Sometimes during my trips to Pittsburgh I rented a pillow from the porter and slept during the night. In the morning when the train pulled into the Pittsburgh Station, I phoned Aunt Dora, and either cousin Bob or cousin Phil drove to the station and brought me to their home at 5528 Bartlett Street in Squirrel Hill, a suburb of Pittsburgh.

Aunt Dora, Uncle Ben and their three grown children lived in a large attached two-story house which they rented from the landlord, who lived next door. The house was fronted by a grass lawn and had a small backyard where Aunt Dora had flowers and tomato plants bordering the grass lawn.

The family also had a live-in maid named Katherine, who worked for them for many years until she got married and moved away to start her own family. My assigned bedroom was on the third floor, which was part of the attic.

During the summer months the attic became very hot, but I

didn't mind. Most homes in Squirrel Hill did not have air conditioning, so electric fans were used to fend off the summer heat. There was a minute fan in my attic bedroom, which made the heat bearable. My activities in Aunt Dora's house included mowing the lawns, going to the movies on Murray Avenue, and reading. Uncle Ben and Bob went work every day to the Rapid Springs Company, a small factory owned by Uncle Ben. The company made products out of wire, such as wire lawn staples used for croquet games and springs used to clear clogs in pipes, often called "snakes."

My cousin Phil went to work as a writer for Radio Station KDKA, and Janet worked as a social worker. Aunt Dora did not have a job, but she was a member of several organizations, such as the Women's Auxiliary of the American Legion and other volunteer organizations which kept her busy most of the time. Therefore, I was pretty much left alone for most weekdays.

When they weren't working, the family tried its best to keep me amused. Once Bob played catch with me in a nearby park. He threw me grounders and then pretended he was a baseball announcer. I was the short stop and he was the first baseman.

"It's a sharply hit grounder to the short stop; Larry fields it cleanly and tosses the ball to first base for the first out." I enjoyed playing with my cousin Bob, but unfortunately Bob was a bit out of shape, and all this exercise gave him a sore arm and back.

That was the last baseball game he announced that summer. However, he did take me to see the Pittsburgh Pirates play a night game at Forbes Field, which was the first night game I ever saw. I was amazed at how bright they could make the field look when it was dark outside. My cousin Phil also related to me when he had the chance. He took me to watch him play tennis, and he also tried to interest me in the piano. The family owned a Steinway Grand Piano which was placed in the living room.

Phil taught me to play "Girl of My Dreams" with one finger. I mastered that by memorizing the keys, but I did not have the talent for going any further by learning to read the notes.

Even Katherine, the family maid, did her part in keeping me busy. She showed me how to make root beer and let me mix the mixture of water, sugar, yeast and root beer extract made by the Hires Company. When the glass bottles were filled by using a funnel, they were capped with a rubber stopper which was held tightly by a wire spring and then taken to the basement to ferment. In a few days the root beer was ready to drink. The spring top would be loosened, the cork would open with a loud champagne-like "pop" and a puff of smoke would arise from the narrow neck of the bottle. The taste of this home-made root beer was the best I have ever had. To this day my favorite soft drink is root beer, but no commercially made root beer can ever compare to the kind that Katherine and I made together.

While all these activities kept me busy and happy, there were still lots of times during the day when I was alone and had little to do. True, I could mow and water the lawns in front and back, but those chores didn't last long. The Davis family must have been aware of this situation, because there was a big change during my next summer visit.

Apparently my summer holiday in Pittsburgh was a success all around. I was pretty well behaved and loved being around a complete family, who loved one another and got along well with everyone, including me. Aunt Lillie and Grandma were relieved of the burden of taking care of me for a few months, so the experiment was deemed a success. The following summer it was decided to repeat my visit to Pittsburgh, and it was repeated the next year, too.

During my next summer with the Davis Family in Pittsburgh, my host family decided to enroll me in the day camp program at the local YMHA. This was a whole new ball game for me. I was placed with a group of boys my own age, and we played games all day long. There was softball (they called it "mush ball," because the ball was bigger and softer than a regular baseball), and basketball in a large gym.

There was a swimming pool where I learned how to swim. There were arts and crafts where I was taught how to make rings with small beads strung onto thin wire. While at day camp I thrived. Not only did I make friends with the guys in my group, but I related well with the counselors who became father figures to me.

There was a tall, slim counselor with wavy black hair who was my group's counselor named Mark, who was in his early twenties. He was a great counselor and a good role model whom I related to as though he were my older brother or my father. Then there was an older man we called "Ziggy," who also served as a father figure to me.

Finally there was the swimming coach, a young man also in his early twenties with bright blond hair combed back. His name was Paul. My Uncle Ben, who paid my tuition for day camp, may not have realized the dynamics of how well I was relating to these fine young counselors and the "Y" program.

During this summer season, I also met a boy my age who was related to Uncle Ben. His name was Herb Magidson. He lived a few blocks away from Bartlett Street and also went to the "Y" summer day camp. Herb's family consisted of his mother, father, and three sisters, named Helen, Cutie, and Jeanie. (Herb Magidson had an uncle with the same name who was a famous song writer. Among many other songs he wrote the lyrics to "The Continental," a big hit back in those days.)

Herb and I became best friends. We played together in day camp and we hung out after supper in his backyard. Sometimes a friend, whom we called "Horn" because that was his last name, would join us in the backyard. Herb's youngest sister, Jeanie, and his oldest sister, Helen, would also hang out with us.

Herb, Horn, and I were curious and adventurous eleven-year-old boys. Someone got hold of a pack of cigarettes and we decided to try smoking them. Perhaps it was our wish to appear older or just curiosity which prompted us to light up. Helen, the oldest sister, was already a habitual smoker. She did not try to stop our experiment. We coughed and sputtered as we puffed on our first cigarette. Helen noticed that I was not inhaling the cigarette smoke. Helen said to me, "You're not inhaling." "I asked, "How do you inhale?"

"I'm not going to tell you," said Helen. "It's not good for you." No matter how much I pleaded, she refused to show me how to inhale.

Many years later I realized how wise Helen was in refusing to teach me how to inhale. Even though I later smoked cigarettes, pipe tobacco, and cigars, I never inhaled, so my lungs are clear to this day.

CHAPTER SEVEN

Camping out

DURING THE DAY CAMP SEASON at the "Y," another pleasant experience came about without my expecting it. The three counselors, Mark, Ziggy, and Paul, decided to take a group of boys on an overnight camping trip. Herb, Horn, another boy, and I were the lucky ones chosen to go on this trip which was not part of the day camp program. The three counselors would be taking us camping on their own time.

To this day, more than seventy years later, I still remember going camping for the first time in my life and enjoying every minute of it, although I don't remember many of the details of what we did on that trip. I do remember cooking our own meals on a campfire, roasting marshmallows and sleeping under a starry sky.

I suppose when the three counselors planned this camping trip, they thought that the boys would enjoy it, but little did they know how much it meant to me. It was like what the poet Longfellow said when he expressed the idea that we may not realize the full extent of our actions. In the poem, "The Arrow and the Song," he wrote: "I shot an arrow into the air / It fell to earth, I know not where." Perhaps it was the arrow that these three generous counselors launched that influenced me to become a day camp counselor later in my life.

Again, my visit to Pittsburgh that summer was deemed a success and the next summer I was allowed to repeat my trip. Once more Uncle Ben enrolled me into the "Y" day camp program. When I arrived at the "Y" on the first day, I saw my favorite counselor, Mark, standing outside in front of the "Y." I greeted him by running toward him and hugging him as though he were part of my family. I was beginning to experience continuity in my life, and seeing Mark again gave me a sense of security that I had longed for most of my life.

The program that summer was very similar to the previous summer's, and I enjoyed it as much as I did before. In the evenings we again hung out in Herb's back yard. Then the "Y" program ended in late August, and I prepared for my journey back to New York. My feelings of security and continuity, however, did not last when I returned to my home on Bennett Avenue.

Chapter Eight

A suitable family

IT SEEMED THAT MY FATHER HAD found a job as a sales clerk in a liquor store at the corner of 50th Street and 8th Avenue working for a man named I.M. Goldberg. This good news prompted Aunt Lillie and Grandma to urge my father to resume the responsibility for my care, even if it meant paying a family to take care of me. My father couldn't argue against the plan because my grandparents, Aunt Lillie, and Aunt Dora had done their best to take care of me for a number of years. The only problem that remained was how to find a suitable family to take care of a 12-year-old boy who wanted a stable family life.

The answer to this problem soon came in the form of Aunt Eva and Uncle Harry, who were living with their two sons, Oscar and Allen, in an apartment on 192nd Street and Broadway. Only this family couldn't take me into their home because it was too miniscule for another child. But Aunt Eva knew of a family two floors down from their apartment who would be interested in caring for me if my father would pay for my room and board.

And so the deal was struck. Without any farewell ceremonies, I left my home on Bennett Avenue and became the ward of an elderly widow named Rose Herman and her grown son Melvin.

I don't remember how I got to the home of the Herman family, but I do remember going to sleep on a double sofa bed in the living room and waking up with a man sleeping next to me.

As I started getting up, the man next to me arose and said, "Hello, my name is Melvin. What's yours?" Shyly I told him my name. Together Melvin and I made the bed and folded it back into its couch position.

Melvin turned out to be a kind, older brother. He taught me many things, such as how to take a shower in under three minutes.

He used a stop watch to time me.

When I told him I was having trouble hitting the baseball during our baseball games in the empty lot on Bennett Avenue, he showed me how to stand and swing the bat. Each night when he returned from work during the baseball season, he would ask me, "How many hits did you get today?" I would tell him, but often I exaggerated my prowess with the bat, just to please him.

Melvin, who was in his mid-20s, seemed tall to me; he had a square shape to his face and blue eyes. His dark brown hair was neatly trimmed. His posture was erect, like a soldier standing at attention. In fact, he was a member of the National Guard and often went to drill in a nearby armory.

He used his guard training to play a game with me by pretending I too, was a soldier. In the morning after I had my three-minute shower and got dressed, there would be an inspection. He was the captain and I was a private who would stand at attention while he inspected me up and down, including my finger nails. If I passed inspection, I was awarded a certain number of points called "merits." If something was wrong, like dirt under my fingernails, I was given a "demerit." I rather liked playing this game with Melvin because he spent so much time with me and really cared about me; he was the ideal brother I never had.

Melvin's mother, whom I called "Aunt Rose," also related well with me. She not only cooked for me and sewed on my missing shirt buttons, but she was interested in what went on at school. One day I came home in a panic because I was in a school play and needed some sort of a costume to make me look like a rabbit. Aunt Rose called in a friend and the two of them sewed a pair of rabbit ears from some scraps of material. My stage debut as a rabbit was a success.

The Herman family did not have much money, which was the reason they agreed to take on the burden for my care, but they found ways to take me to cultural events that were free. I remember going to a play in a church called, *Turn to the Right*, which had as its theme the notion that making decisions involves moral choices, and one should always choose the path that is right in a moral or religious context. The theme of the play did not impress me as much as the staging, lighting, scenery and the actors' ability to project their voices to the audience. This was my first experience in seeing a real play, so maybe my subsequent love for theater was born on that little church stage where Aunt Rose took me one night.

As it turned out, the move to the Herman family on 190th Street and Broadway was not as wrenching as I had feared. Not only were Aunt Rose and Melvin gentle and caring foster parents, but I was not far away from my former neighborhood on Bennett Avenue, and it was near enough to my school on Wadsworth Avenue so that I did not have to change schools.

After school, I would drop off my books in the apartment at 192nd Street and walk to my old neighborhood and play with my friends. When darkness descended, I would walk back to 192nd Street and be in time for supper with Aunt Rose and Melvin.

The reason I liked Bennett Avenue is that it was full of kids my age and we always had interesting things to do with each other. Our after-school play activities were coordinated by what we kids called "seasons."

There was the marble season when all the kids brought out their marbles and we played games using marbles. Some kids made up a game with wooden cheese boxes. In those days Philadelphia Brand Cream Cheese came to the dairy in wooden boxes. When the individual packages of cream cheese were all sold, the dairymen threw out the wooden boxes, which we immediately collected from the trash.

Using a miniature saw, some of the kids cut various sized gaps in the side of the wooden cheese box. The gaps looked like small doors through which we could roll our marbles. If we succeeded in rolling a marble from a determined distance through the biggest "door," we would collect one marble from the game operator; if we rolled our marble through a smaller door, we would collect three marbles from the game operator.

The number of marbles we would collect varied inversely with the size of the door cut into the cheese box. More often than not, we failed to roll our marble through any sized hole, and the owner of the game got to keep all the marbles that missed.

After marble season came checkers season, and all the kids on the block brought out their checkers. Instead of playing the traditional game of checkers, we played a game called "Skelley." To this day I still do not know the derivation of the game's name, but we accepted it without question.

For the game of "Skelley," we drew a large square in chalk on the sidewalk, and around the four sides of the square we drew smaller boxes with numbers in each one. The numbers were not in consecutive order or near one another so that a player had to shoot his checker from one side of the square to the other to go from number one to number two. There was a box in the middle of the square, which represented the last box in the game.

The object of the game was to "shoot" our checker with our thumb and forefinger or index finger into each numbered box until we landed in the middle box and won the game. Whoever landed his checker in all the squares first was declared the winner, who then collected a checker from each player. We could play this game for hours.

Then for some unknown reason, the checker season would vanish, and the top season would begin. Every kid showed up with top and string to spin tops on the sidewalk. Some kids had their tops and string ready from last season. If not, the owner of the candy store on the corner would be happy to sell them a new set. The string, which had a button attached on one end, was used to wrap tightly around the top. The button was held between the index and the middle fingers.

To spin the top we would thrust it downward toward the sidewalk, and as the string unwound, it would provide the spin to the top which would land on the steel point of the top. The button, held between the fingers helped the spinner to keep the string taut, which increased the spin. Some tops, the more expensive ones, had a small ball bearing at the small end of the top, which served to keep the top spinning faster and longer.

With our tops we played a game called, "Keep the Kettle Boiling," the object of which was to always have one top spinning in the designated area of our game. When one spinning top was about to lose its speed and topple to the ground, another spinning top had to replace it before the former top stopped spinning. Sometimes a player would fail in his attempt to spin his top; then we would have to start a new game. We could also play at this game for hours.

Eventually, the top season faded away and baseball card season would begin. Baseball cards, which are still in use today, had a picture of a baseball player on one side and the player's biography or "stats" on the other side.

We would trade them with other kids usually when we had two or more copies of one player and wanted another player's card to complete our set. When I grew older and had children of my own, I watched my own son, Phil, as he traded baseball cards with his friend. The two boys would each hold a large stack of cards. Phil's friend would show his cards in rapid succession. As each card was shown, Phil would call out, "Got it, need it, got it need it, etc." "Got it" meant that Phil already had that card and "Need it" meant that he didn't have the card and wanted to trade for it. Then the two boys would reverse roles and Phil's friend would tell Phil what cards he had and what cards he needed.

However, when I was a young boy we not only traded cards, we played for them. One game involved tossing a card from a designated distance toward the wall of an apartment building. The object of the game was to make your card touch another card which had been thrown previously. When a player succeeded in doing this, he won all the cards that were on the ground. Then a new game would start. Another game involved matching. The picture side of the card was called "heads," and the reverse side was called "tails."

One player would flip five or six cards toward the ground. The cards would land showing either "heads" or "tails." The second player had to match the exact number of "heads" and "tails" of the first player by flipping his cards to the ground. If the second player succeeded in matching the cards, he would win all the cards. If he failed to do so, the other player picked up all the cards.

In this game, I usually won more often than I lost because I practiced at home for hours flipping the cards onto the floor until I could control the number of rotations the card made as it flipped onto the floor. In that way I could make the cards land as "heads" or "tails" at will. Of course my opponent also tried to control the cards in the same way, but I had devoted so much time in perfecting my skill that I won almost every time.

As a result of winning all these baseball cards, I amassed several large stacks of cards which I secured with a rubber band and stored in a shoebox. Then I stashed the vast collection of cards under my bed. When I returned from one of my summer trips to Pittsburgh, my baseball cards were gone. Apparently, they had become a victim of someone's housecleaning zeal. I searched for my treasure all over the house, but it was nowhere to be found. I felt that the confiscation of my cards was unnecessary and that my rights had been violated, but there was nothing I could do.

However, I learned from this event that life goes on, and so I returned to my games on Bennett Avenue. From three-thirty in the afternoon to sundown we played our games. When it grew dark, we went home. In essence we depended on the sun to signal us to go home because none of us kids had a watch. A watch was something that only grown-ups wore.

In the winter months using sunset as our clock served us well. It started turning dark around four-thirty or five o'clock. However, in spring the daylight hours increased, and it didn't get dark until six or six-thirty. It did not occur to me that if I wanted to be home at six o'clock for supper at the Herman household, I would have to leave Bennett Avenue before sundown during spring and summer. This miscalculation got me into trouble with my foster parents who liked to eat dinner at 6 p.m. sharp.

One night I arrived at home at 6:30, just as it *was* turning dark. The Hermans had already eaten and were quite upset with me for keeping them waiting and also causing them to worry about me. Melvin gave me several demerits for showing up late. From that time on, I no longer depended on the sun as my watch. Instead I would frequently approach an adult who usually had a wrist watch and ask, "Mister, do you have the time?" I was never late for supper again.

While living with the Hermans, I became friends with my cousin Allen who lived on the fourth floor of our apartment house. He was several years older than I, but we still enjoyed each other's company. At times I visited him in his room just to talk and hang out.

One day Allen told me about a job he had delivering newspapers on Sundays. He worked for a man named Henry who ran a newsstand in front of the subway station on 180th Street, a stone's throw away from our empty lot on Bennett Avenue. Allen said that he wanted to give up the job because he was tired of getting up so early on Sunday. "Would you like the job?" he asked. Since I could use some extra pocket money, I said, "Sure, I'll take the job, if it's okay with Henry."

That Friday afternoon my cousin Allen took me to see Henry who turned out to be a middle-aged man with a ruddy complexion. The toll from eking out a living from a newsstand showed in his lined face. He gave me a friendly greeting and explained what the Sunday morning job entailed.

A list of subscribers to the Sunday *New York Times*, their addresses and apartment numbers would be found inside the newsstand on Sunday morning. I was to place the newspapers in front of each apartment door. I didn't have to collect any money, so I didn't have to ring the bell. All I had to do was place the paper down and leave. For this work I would receive a very modest salary (I forget how much money was involved). In addition, there would be some leftover papers which I could sell at his newsstand and keep all the money from those sales. I agreed immediately and Henry gave me the key to the lock in his newsstand.

We shook hands and then Henry took out three cola bottles

from a case on the floor of his stand. He took the caps off the bottles with an opener and asked Allen and me to tell him what we thought of this new cola drink, which had just come onto the market. Even though the cola was warm, it had a taste similar to the Coca-Cola drink I was used to. It was not the same as the familiar soft drink, but it was close enough. Not only was the cola sweet and fizzy, but it came in a twelve-ounce bottle instead of the six-ounce bottle used by Coca-Cola, which at that time used the phrase, "The Pause that Refreshes" to advertise its product.

The new cola turned out to be Pepsi-Cola, a cola company that challenged Coca-Cola for supremacy in the cola market. Their marketing strategy was simple and clever: they would charge the same price for their cola as Coca-Cola, five cents a bottle, but they would offer twice as much cola, twelve ounces, instead of six. Soon the radios were announcing the campaign of a newcomer to the cola market with a jingle.

As Henry, Allen and I downed our drinks of the new cola, we never thought that we were one of the first to have tasted a cola which would become a giant in the field.

As it turned out, the job of delivering papers early on a Sunday morning was not as lucrative for me as I had hoped. After delivering all the papers on my list, I was left with a dozen papers to sell to people who were taking the subway early Sunday morning. However, few people came to this particular subway station on a Sunday morning and of those few who were traveling, only one or two wanted to buy a paper. I would stay at the stand until noon and my total intake would be 50 or 75 cents. So I stuck it out for four or five weeks and then I returned the key to Henry and made up some excuse for quitting the job.

CHAPTER NINE

Moving again

JUST AS I WAS BEGINNING to adjust to my foster home with the Herman family, I received some bad news. My father had fallen behind in his payments to the Hermans, and there was a quarrel about how much money was owed to Rose Herman for my room and board. Rather than pay the money that was owed, my father decided to terminate the arrangement, so back I went to the apartment on Bennett Avenue.

However, I was only to stay there until another arrangement could be made with another family that would consent to take me in. I don't remember the family name of the couple that was chosen as my next caregivers, but I do remember their first names: they were Helga and Swen, a couple who had emigrated from Sweden with their two daughters.

Swen was a kind gentleman in his 40s who still had traces of a Swedish accent. His wife, Helga, was soft-spoken. She had gray hair and wore glasses. Besides their two daughters, the family had two other children whom they were caring for: a tall girl, slightly older than I, and a younger, frail-looking boy whose mother was divorced. This Swedish family supplemented their income by taking in children whose parents, for one reason or another, could not maintain them on their own. The family had a large apartment on Fort Washington Avenue, not too far from our apartment on Bennett Avenue. So again, I didn't have to change schools as I moved into a new home and became part of a new family.

While I was never a part of the planning that determined where I was to live and with whom, I inferred that the family must have decided that not only I was to live with this family, but it was time for me to be reunited with my sister, Esther Ruth, who had been living in Pittsburgh with Aunt Dora and Uncle Ben. So Esther

Ruth and I were given a room to ourselves in this large apartment. It was hoped, I suppose, that reuniting Esther Ruth and me would create a close bond between us, but it did not turn out that way. We had been separated for too long, and I had developed a defense mechanism that could be expressed as: "No one else cares about you, so you had better look out for yourself."

Esther Ruth, on the other hand, had flourished while living with Aunt Dora, Uncle Ben, and her grown cousins, Bob, Phil, and Janet. As the youngest child in the family, she had been catered to and not much was demanded of her. Therefore, bringing these two personalities together did not accomplish the closeness for which the family had hoped. We did play together and quarreled as normal brothers and sisters do, but we had not bonded because we had so little history together. I was cast as the older brother who would look out for his younger sister, but I refused to play my part. As a result, my sister and I tolerated each other, but we never grew close.

Life with our Swedish-American family was good and wholesome. My sister and I learned to get along with our adoptive parents and with the other children. We had evening meals together and enjoyed wholesome and well-cooked food prepared by Helga.

While living with this foster family there were two incidents which made an impression on me. The first one involved my misbehavior at school. The loss of my real family life with a mother, father and sisters had taken its toll on me. I longed for the stability of a family life which many of my friends took for granted. As a result I began acting out in school, trying to draw attention to myself. I would interrupt the teacher's lesson by calling out and trying to crack jokes. I whispered to those around me when I should have been listening. I also would shoot wads of paper with a rubber band at the necks of children in front of me. In short, I was out of control.

Finally my sixth grade teacher had enough of my pranks and interruptions. She must have discussed my behavior with the principal because after one of my antics, the teacher wrote a note to my mother asking for a meeting. She told me that I was to go home and not return until she had seen one of my parents.

I was devastated. To be sent home in disgrace was bad enough, but getting my parents involved was even worse for me. How could I get my mother to come to school? She was in a state hospital in Cleveland. My father couldn't come to school, either, because he had to work. I had really dug a hole for myself and I had no family who could get me out of it.

Therefore, I took my teacher's note to the only family I knew and showed it tearfully to Helga. She read the note carefully and talked to me quietly. She didn't scold me or tell me how foolish I had been, but rather she identified with my anxiety about being suspended from school and my being unable to meet the teacher's demands for my return. Helga told me that she and her husband would figure out something to relieve me of my predicament.

When Swen came home, he was informed of my problem, and the three of us, Helga, Swen and I decided what to do. I would promise to behave in class, and my foster parents would write a note explaining the reasons why my real parents could not come to school. They also wrote that I had promised them never to misbehave in class again. They closed the letter by asking the teacher to allow me to rejoin the class.

The next day the teacher read the note and I was allowed to return to my classmates. From that day on, I kept my promise not to misbehave to the best of my ability. Recognizing that it was part of my nature to be humorous, the teacher made a deal with me by allowing me two bursts of humor a day and no more. I kept my part of the bargain, and we got along well for the rest of the term.

Not only do I remember the teacher's role in dealing with my misconduct, but I also recall how sensitively my foster parents handled the situation. They didn't scold me or call me a rotten kid. Instead, they helped me learn that some conduct is unacceptable and how I could remedy my predicament.

The other memory was not as emotional as the first. It

involved a pet dog that from time to time visited with the little boy whose parents were divorced. His mother visited him frequently and brought with her the strangest dog I had ever seen. It was called a Mexican Hairless, which referred to the dog's lack of hair or skin covering. Its exposed skin was gray like an elephant's, and it had a tiny tuft of white hair on its head and some on its tail.

Otherwise, as its name suggests, it was completely bald. The dog, whose name was "Poncho," was, very nervous and could barely sit still when he was around people. He would offer himself for petting whenever anyone came near him. Poncho was a dog who loved to be loved. While people were his first love, going outside for a walk or run was second on his wish list. If one asked Poncho, "Do you want to go out?" the dog would raise his ears, run to the door and jump up to the door knob. Then he would race back to the person who had asked the question as if to say, "I'm ready. What's keeping you?" Poncho would repeat these actions until someone would get his leash, attach it to his collar, and take him out.

In the house, Poncho would lie down on a rug, but only if no human was around. Otherwise, he would jump on a sitting person's lap, even a strange visitor's. Sometimes his offer to cuddle with someone would be rejected. In that case he would jump back to the floor and offer himself to another seated person, or he would be content to lie down on his favorite spot on the rug.

The reason I know so much about Poncho is that he was eventually adopted by Aunt Lillie when the divorced woman said she could no longer care for this strange-looking dog. It was a good match: a dog and a woman who both needed unconditional love.

While I stayed with Aunt Lillie, I had the job of taking Poncho for a walk several times a day. In return, Poncho would jump on my lap, lick my face and give some of his huge store of love to me. Aunt Lillie loved that dog until the day he died of old age.

Life with the Swedish family and their wards was running smoothly for my sister and me when history repeated itself. According to the philosopher, Santayana, "those who cannot learn from the past are condemned to repeat it."

Once again my father could not or would not make the necessary payments for our upkeep, so we had to say good-bye to Helga, Swen, their biological children and their adopted ones. Sadly we returned to our former homes. Esther Ruth went back to Pittsburgh to resume her life with Aunt Dora and family and I returned to Aunt Lillie and Grandma Fanny.

CHAPTER TEN
Junior high school

THE MOVE TO 370 RIVERSIDE DRIVE on 109th Street also brought me to Junior High School 165 Manhattan, located on 109th Street between Broadway and Amsterdam Avenue. J.H.S. 165 taught students from grades seven through nine. Our curriculum took us to various teachers for forty-five minutes at a time. We traveled to our teachers' rooms as a class and met each morning with our homeroom teacher who took attendance and often taught one of the subjects in the curriculum.

A few teachers stand out in my memory of those days. One such teacher was a rather large woman with a booming voice and a German accent who tried to drum French into a mostly unwilling group of students. Mrs. Blankenship was a devoted teacher who was bent on pounding some knowledge of the French language into our all but closed minds. She was a massive woman with white hair and glasses who was on a never-ending diet. For lunch she ate a large navel orange which one of her students bought for her at a neighborhood grocery store. Her bearing was almost military as she kept would-be trouble-makers in line and taught them French, whether they liked it or not.

What surprised us the most about Mrs. Blankenship was that so many students wound up liking her despite her fierce demeanor. Toward the end of the term, when high school students had some time off from school, her former students would visit her and tell her how they were doing in high school. As these big hulking students entered her classroom, she welcomed the interruption and greeted each visitor by name. During these brief visits from her former students, Mrs. Blankenship discarded her "no-nonsense" manner and revealed her true nature of a dedicated teacher who loved her work and cared for her students.

I also remember our social studies teacher who was as fond of apples as Mrs. Blankenship was fond of oranges. However, Mr. Crooker could not wait until lunchtime to eat his favorite fruit, so he ate them in class and invited his students to do the same. Every day that we had social studies with this unorthodox teacher, we brought all kinds of apples to munch while we discussed current events and argued with one another about government policies and politics in general.

One fall day after Mr. Crooker had visited an apple orchard in upstate New York, he brought a whole bushel basket of apples to class and invited us to help ourselves to those bright red Macintosh apples.

I had never heard of algebra until I got promoted to this ninth grade class. One day Mrs. Sands announced that there would be a test in algebra the next day. I was stunned and feared that I would flunk the test and be placed in a slower class. I didn't know what to do. Fortunately we had a textbook that presented many examples in algebra and also had the answers to the examples in the back of the book. Then it occurred to me that if I started with the answers and worked backwards, I could figure out the steps that it took to arrive at the answer. I worked with the examples all afternoon.

After supper I worked late into the night. First I started with the answer to an example in the back of the book. Then I found out the steps needed to arrive at the answer. Once I knew the process, I could start with the examples and check my answers with those in the back of the book. In short, I had taught myself algebra in one afternoon and evening. The next day I aced the test and learned that I could succeed in this class of bright children if I worked hard enough.

Mrs. Sands knew that she had to keep challenging her class. She used to say she needed to stretch our minds lest we become complacent. One day she told us she had received permission from the principal and the commercial department in our school to teach us typing.

"Typing?" we asked. "Wasn't typing something for the

commercial students?"

"Yes," she replied, "typing is something that commercial students take as part of their curriculum. But that doesn't mean general students like you wouldn't benefit from knowing how to touch type. It's a skill that you will need for the rest of your life."

It didn't take long for Mrs. Sands to convince us so the next day we went into the typing class at a time when it wasn't being used by the commercial students.

The typing class consisted of thirty or so desks with a Remington typewriter atop each desk. These typewriters were a bit unusual since there were no letters marked on the keys. Each student was given a typing book which showed us the letters each key represented.

Mrs. Sands taught us how to hold our hands over the keyboard as if we were about to play a piano. Our fingers were to rest on the home keys with the left pinky on the "a" key, the next left hand finger on the "s" key, and so on. For the right hand, the index finger should be on the "j," the middle finger was to be on the "k," and so on.

The art of touch typing was to assign each letter and symbol to a certain finger and to always use only that finger when typing that particular letter. Both thumbs were used for the space bar. The exercise book gave us practice in typing each letter with its assigned finger without looking at the keys.

For example, we would type one row of "aaa, aaa, aaa," etc. Then we would type one row of "sss, sss, sss," etc. Soon were typing words and then sentences. By the end of four or five weeks we could type whole paragraphs or business letters without looking at the keys.

Of course we were not as fast as the commercial students at typing but our speed picked up as we practiced more and more.

Today, more than seventy years later, I still use touch typing the way Mrs. Sands taught us. How wise was Mrs. Sands to teach us a skill which we could use for a lifetime.

Since Mrs. Sands' class had been together for more than two

years, friendships had long been established and, as the new student, I didn't know anyone. Then the class clown named Laurie Seidman came to my rescue. He approached me the first day I was in class and introduced himself to me with a broad smile on his face. Then he introduced me to some of his friends and made me feel at home. He appeared to be always laughing and finding humor in every situation. Having once been a class clown myself, I appreciated his ability to make people laugh. Laurie and I quickly became good friends.

At that time Laurie lived on 110th Street just east of Broadway. He often invited me to his apartment to listen to his 78 rpm records of the swing bands like Benny Goodman, Artie Shaw, Tommy and Jimmy Dorsey and many other bands. He had a vast collection of records with labels like Decca, RCA, and Columbia. We would spend hours in his room listening to his latest records. While visiting I met his father, Leo, his mother, Ida, his older brother, Nat, and his older sister, Sybil. They seemed to me to be the perfect family and I wished I had one like that. Sometimes Laurie would invite me to stay for dinner. When I accepted, he would say to his mother, "Ida, Larry's staying for dinner. Throw another carrot in the soup." His mother would smile and make me feel welcome.

Although the Seidmans were Jewish, they celebrated Christmas because they liked the idea of exchanging gifts. They even had a little Christmas tree in their apartment. One Christmas day I was invited to their apartment and I watched as they opened their Christmas gifts. Laurie's older brother, Nat, came over to me and handed me a beautifully wrapped box which contained a silk tie. I was at once surprised and so pleased for I rarely received presents from my own family, and certainly not at Christmas time. It was just not part of the family's tradition to give each other presents. I don't even remember their saying "Happy Birthday" to anyone on his or her birthday, let alone having a cake with candles or a present for the person having a birthday. That is why I was so touched when Nat handed me a gift with my name on it.

Laurie was prone to share his ideas and prospects. He joined a Zionist group that played basketball in a local school gymnasium, and invited me to join him. I did so, and enjoyed playing once a week.

Whenever Laurie had an idea for an activity, he invited me to come along. It was not surprising, therefore, that when Laurie invited me to join his Boy Scout group, I readily consented.

The troop, Number 566 Manhattan, met on Friday evenings in the inside yard of our local junior high school. The troop was divided into several groups called patrols, headed by a patrol leader. Our patrol was named the "Bull Moose" patrol, probably because the animal is big and strong and a kind of leader of the pack. Our activities each Friday night consisted of mastering certain skills in order to advance in rank and to amass "merit badges," which also helped us to advance in rank. The ranks, as far as I can remember, are: Tenderfoot, Second Class, First Class, Star, Life and Eagle. I believe I worked my way up to Star Scout when I decided to leave scouting and concentrate on my school work for I hoped to get into City College when I graduated high school.

The skills we worked on were those one needed in the outdoors as well as in everyday living, such as rope-tying, first aid, fire-building with flint and steel, bow and drill, and Morse code signaling. Laurie and I were a team. I sent the Morse code by waving a flag and Laurie tried his best to receive and write down the message.

Skills that could not be demonstrated in an indoor yard were developed in the outdoors on hikes which took place on Saturdays in Van Courtland Park. Here we would take a seven-mile walk into the park, stop for lunch, build a fire using only one match, and cook our meal. After lunch we played games in Van Cortland Park and then walked back another seven miles to complete our fourteen-mile hike. Before heading home on the subway, we would stop in the "White Castle" and consume a number of hamburgers with chopped onions and a slice of pickle. They were delicious and only cost five cents each.

Our patrol system was governed by competition, so points were allotted for winning a competition on one of the skills described earlier; points were also awarded for participation in Saturday hikes or for passing tests or achieving the next rank in scouting. Each troop was supposed to be run by a scout master. Ours was named Arthur Corson, but he was an absentee scout master, so the troop was actually run by high school seniors who were devoted role models and did a fine job. Their names were Paul Ragusis, William Ruder, Richard Bernstein, and Irwin Kleiner. These assistant scout masters accompanied us on hikes, and during the summer went with us to sleep-away camp.

Once in a while our absentee scout master showed up and ruined everything. He was like a marine sergeant who thought we were having too much fun. He made us stand at attention while he scolded us for not being serious about scouting. Then he made us march up and down the school yard and drilled us until we got it right. Fortunately he didn't come by very often, and so we enjoyed most of our Friday night meetings. At the end of our meeting, we adjourned to Ike's candy store where we consumed ice cream sodas and played the pinball machine.

One of our activities in our scouting days was to put out a newspaper chronicling our activities during the month. Our paper was called *The Palm Leaf*, which was founded and edited by a clever scout named Leonard Sternfels. Sternfels encouraged each patrol leader to submit articles for the newspaper. As a way of urging my patrol to work harder, because we were in last place in our point system, I submitted the following poem entitled "Last Place."

> *We've been working very hard, and we've set a dizzy pace*
> *So now we're possessors of a noble berth: last place.*
> *The sweat which fell from all our brows*
> *Has formed a slippery base, and the cry that you hear now*
> *Is "We slipped into last place."*
> *You might think we are selfish, but that is not the case.*

You might have anything you wish, except, of course,
    LAST PLACE.
We've done nothing all year long, for we're a bunch of aces.
We just sit and sing a song, which tells how nice last place is.

All in all, scouting was a good experience for most of us and some of the friendships formed there lasted a lifetime. Usually friendships develop as a result of close associations in some enterprise like school, camp, work or living in the same neighborhood. When these activities end, the relationships usually end also. However, at times, the relationships formed are so strong that friends try their best to "keep in touch," and if the geographic distance is not too great, the friendship continues on another, deeper level.

When we grew older and started dating girls, we double and triple dated. After World War II, we went to one another's weddings. Laurie was best man when I married Celia Grossman. I, in turn, attended Laurie's ceremony when he married Mimie Nestler.

I was friends with Laurie Seidman until the day he died. Milton Kalin (Kuzy) is still a good friend who lives on Long Island and several years ago I got in touch with Dick Hyman, who was also in our troop and a close friend to Laurie and Kuzy.

Today in some quarters scouting has a somewhat tarnished image. There is a joke about the Boy Scout who, anxious to perform his daily good deed, grabs the arm of a blind woman and takes her across the street. The woman, instead of thanking the Scout, complains, "But I didn't want to cross the street."

However, when I was twelve, thirteen and fourteen years of age, scouting was an activity which channeled our energies into wholesome activities and fostered lasting friendships. Someday someone might do a study which follows the lives of boys and girls who made scouting a part of their lives. The hypothesis of the study would be that scouting contributes to a successful and happy life. My friend, Laurie, for example, was happily married, and raised a family of three children. He became an elementary school teacher and then a college professor of social studies at C.W. Post in Long Island. Milton Kalin (Kuzy) was also successfully married, raised a fine family and became the head of his own guidance center. Dick Hyman married his long-time sweetheart, became an industrial engineer and worked for the same aircraft builder for his entire career. This is not to say that scouting alone contributed to the stability of these lives, but it may have played an important role.

If meeting indoors every Friday evening played an important part in our ability to foster and maintain relationships, then attending summer sleep-away camp played an even greater role. One day a notice arrived in the mail addressed to me. It announced the fact that the Boy Scouts were accepting reservations for their summer camp at Ten Mile River. Everyone in the troop received the notice, and at our next meeting, I found out that most of my friends in the troop planned to attend summer camp.

My family, Aunt Lillie and Grandma, did not believe in what they called "frills." They inherited a depression psychology which caused them to place expenses into two categories: "necessities" and "frills." Summer camp was definitely not a "necessity" in their economics. An item in the "necessity" column would be a winter coat, which calls up another memory.

Someone gave me a dime bank when I was living with my grandparents and Aunt Lillie. It was a slender, shiny cylinder with a circumference not much bigger than a dime. It held only dimes, ten dollars worth when it was completely full. Somehow over a year's time I saved up one hundred dimes in my tiny dime bank. I had no idea what I would do with my ten dollars, but buying a winter coat was not on the top of the list. However, my family had a list of their own for that money and buying me a winter coat *was* at the top of their list. No amount of pleading or crying or pointing out how unfair it was to take the money I had saved so diligently could dissuade my family, including my own father, from using my own money as partial payment for the coat. The coat that was bought was warm, lined with sheep's wool, but it was not my idea of how my own money should be spent.

But this was an example of how my family handled their expenses. How in the world could I convince my family to spend money on such a frill as summer camp? I had one argument in my favor, however. The cost of a two-week stay at Ten Mile River was only fourteen dollars. The low price set by the Boy Scouts was meant to allow children whose families could not otherwise afford it, to attend camp for a brief period. Secondly, the prospect of not having to feed me or put up with my shenanigans for a whole two weeks may have tipped the scales in my favor, for they consented to write the check for fourteen dollars and send it along with my application.

In the first week of July, I boarded a bus with my troop buddies bound for the Ten Mile River Boy Scout Camp. We must have been a noisy bunch for the poor bus driver who had to listen to songs about the fate of 100 bottles of beer on the wall, some farmer named MacDonald and his noisy animals, and some railroad worker whose wife was named Dinah. At the half-way point we made a stop at the "Red Apple Rest Stop" where we used the bathroom facilities and bought as much candy and soda as our pocket money would allow. Then we continued our trip to camp. Two weeks seemed like a long time when we started, but we had so much fun together that the time seemed to slide by like the sand through an hour glass.

During this short period of time, I managed to get a severe sunburn on my back, because I played basketball with my shirt and undershirt off in the hot blazing sun for an hour or so. I learned how to weave a lanyard out of strips of plastic. Laurie and I passed our mapping skills test by making a map to scale of an area of the camp. We participated in a treasure hunt in which clues were given on index cards which took us all over the camp.

Later in life I would use the treasure hunt principles to challenge my son Steve on his birthday, and later still I made treasure hunts for my grandchildren.

Our meals in the mess hall were also memorable. We sat ten or twelve to a table with a counselor at each table to ensure some kind of eating decorum. We were served family style by waiters who were older campers. After devouring huge quantities of food, we took turns in a clean-up ritual which involved wiping plates as clean as possible with paper napkins so that the dishwashing machine could then wash the dishes.

We played baseball games against other troops. I was the pitcher in one game which was very close up until the ninth inning. Our team was ahead by one run and our opponents had two outs and the bases loaded. They were loaded because I had walked three batters in a row. I had a wicked slider which sank low and wide from a right-handed hitter.

The other team couldn't hit the pitch, but they discovered that if they just let the pitch go by it would be called a ball. That is why they had three men on base. Their next man up was known as a weak hitter. If I didn't get the ball over the plate for strikes, I could walk in the next runner and the score would be tied with the bases still full. I decided to forget about my slider, and instead, pitch very carefully to the batter in the strike zone. The batter swung at the straight pitch with no speed on it and connected. The ball sailed into the outfield.

All the base runners were on the move and it looked like they would all score. However, my friend Kuzy was back-pedaling as fast as he could go with one hand shading his eyes from the sun's glare and the gloved hand reaching for the fly ball. Somehow he managed to catch the ball and save the game for our team. It was a thrilling moment for everyone.

I also remember the night ceremony for an honor society of the Boy Scouts called "The Order of the Arrow." Outstanding scouts were selected by their scout masters to be inducted into this honor society. Inductees had to undergo an initiation rite which made them remain silent for one whole day before the induction ceremony. The candidate was not allowed to talk to anyone as part of his initiation. At night we sat around a huge unlit bonfire with light only from our flashlights. There was a steel wire going from a high tree above the bonfire to the middle of the logs of the bonfire.

The names of the new members of The Order of the Arrow were called out and then a scout dressed as an American Indian called on the God of Fire to light the way for the new members. In an instant a great ball of fire made up of rags soaked in kerosene descended from the tree guided by the steel wire; it ignited the large stack of logs which made a huge bonfire. All of us were impressed by the ceremony. New members of the order could all wear an arrow pin on their uniforms to signify their membership in this honor society.

Soon the two fun-filled weeks slipped away. One week before the two-week period, I wrote home and asked if my family would stake me for another two weeks, but the request was met with silence. My friend Laurie offered to ask his parents for the money, but I was too proud and I refused his kind offer.

I was sad to leave on that last day, especially since I was the only one from our troop who had to go. That trip was my only experience with sleep-away camp, but it made such an impression on me that I made sure that my own children would have as much sleep-away camp as they wanted, whether it was a Boy Scout Camp or some other camp. I would have liked to remain in scouting for a longer time. Perhaps I could have joined those older high school boys whom I admired so much for their leadership and dedication to scouting activities.

As a patrol leader, I had to attend weekly meetings with the assistant scout masters to plan events for the coming week. Each week we met at someone's house to review last week's activities and to plan for the upcoming week. All of these meetings, the weekly planning session, the Friday night meetings and the Saturday hikes took a great deal of time. As a junior high school student, I had a great deal of time to spare for these scouting activities, but when I reached high school, my time became more limited.

I needed more time to concentrate on my school work because I had a strong desire to attend The City College of New York. In order to accomplish this goal, I had to have a high enough average to qualify. City College charged no tuition, but it limited enrollment to those students who had shown good scholarship in high school. The minimum average for acceptance into the college at that time was eighty-five. I knew that if I worked hard at getting good grades, I could get accepted at the college, but I needed time to study. That is why when I was the host for one of the patrol leader's meetings I announced that I had to quit scouting.

The assistant scout masters and the other patrol leaders tried to get me to change my mind. Dick Bernstein, one of the scout masters, asked, "Is it the uniform that you don't like? We could let you wear long pants instead of knickers if you think you are getting too old for the uniform as it is." "That's not it," I said. "I just need more time to study."

They all tried their best to dissuade me, but I had made up my mind that my goal of attending college was too important. Reluctantly they accepted my decision, and I sadly said farewell to scouting and all it had meant to me.

One might wonder what gave me the idea that going to college was so important. The idea certainly did not come from my family. During the family council meetings, to which I was never invited, it had been decided that I should become some kind of factory worker. Aunt Mamie thought I could make a decent living as a truck driver.

For two years during the summer months I was again shipped off to Pittsburgh and West Virginia, respectively. In Pittsburgh I stayed with Aunt Dora and Uncle Ben and their grown children, Philip, Janet and Bob, but this time it was not to vacation and go to day camp.

This time I was apprenticed to Uncle Ben's "Rapid Spring Company," which made various products out of steel wire, such as lawn staples and wire springs. I proved not to be much of an asset to the company, for Uncle Ben and his son, Bob, didn't need another employee in their three-man factory. Uncle Ben took me on only as a favor to the family. I served as a kind of delivery boy, carrying little packages to the post office and such.

Once they tried to let me work on a machine that stamped out huge wire staples which could be driven into lawns for a game of croquet. The staples were stamped out by the machine and made to slide down an iron railing. My job was to scoop up the staples as they came down the rail with a steel paddle shaped like a spatula and insert them into a cardboard box, so many staples to each box. It sounds like a simple task, but it was not, for the machine worked at a steady pace, but I, who was new at the job, did not.

As a result the machine produced more staples than I could box, and in order to avoid having staples fall to the ground from the over-filled rail, I had to stop the machine. If the machine were human, it would have said, "I don't like to be stopped and started. It ruins my momentum." Even though my cousin Bob demonstrated how to do this job again and again, I still couldn't get the hang of it. I recalled that unforgiving wire machine when I watched an episode of "I Love Lucy" in which Lucy is at a conveyor belt in a chocolate candy factory. Her task was to decorate chocolate candy and place them in a box as they came off the belt. When the conveyor belt was accelerated, Lucy couldn't keep up. Instead of boxing the chocolates, she put them in her mouth, her pockets, and her bra, making for a hilarious scene.

It was not hilarious for me, however, when I couldn't keep pace with even the slowest setting of the wire stamping machine. Since it was not practical to keep stopping and starting the machine, it was decided to relieve me of the task. I was given other menial tasks to perform, but I barely earned my salary of six dollars a week.

As I watched the experienced men work, I noticed that the job was hard, the pay was low, and the satisfaction for the job was minimal. Contrary to my family's expectations, I learned that a job in a factory was one I wanted to avoid at any cost. If I tried to enter the workforce as a beginner with only a high school education, I would be doomed to live the hard life of the workers in my uncle's factory. I learned that I needed more education and more time to think about my future career. My family had wanted to teach me how to adjust to work in a factory; instead they taught me how to hope for something better.

That lesson was reinforced the next summer when I was sent to work in my Uncle Harry's furniture store. Uncle Harry was even less thrilled about having a young kid in his employ than was my Uncle Ben. He even tried to talk me out of working for him. "You can just have a summer vacation and live with us for two months," he said.

I knew, however, that my family wanted me to have more work experience, so I had to refuse the vacation offer. Uncle Harry, not wishing to disappoint his wife, my Aunt Selma, who was in favor of the plan to have me work at the store, finally consented to take me on to work in his warehouse, where I was put to work polishing gas stoves which had become full of soot, dust and animal droppings.

This experience put the final nail in the coffin of any plans to have me work as a hired hand. I could not contemplate working every day of my working life in such an environment. My family had taught me well, even though the lesson learned was not the one they intended.

CHAPTER ELEVEN

A new neighborhood

WHEN FAMILIES CHOOSE A NEIGHBORHOOD to move to, they usually check out the area to see if the surrounding apartment houses are well kept, if the apartment house is near public transportation, and if it is near food markets and shops. My family didn't check to see if there were boys my age with whom I could play. As it turned out our apartment house on 109th Street and Riverside Drive was devoid of kids my age.

There were plenty of older boys, junior and seniors in high school who belonged to an athletic club called "The Royals." They bought uniform blue jackets with the words "Royals A. C." written in cursive writing across the back. Athletic clubs were common in those days, and groups would challenge each other to play baseball or football games, but more often they would just hang out with each other wearing their uniform jackets and looking what later would be regarded as "cool."

Needless to say, these older boys would have nothing to do with younger kids like me. One of the Royals had a younger brother with whom I could play, but aside from him there were few boys my age with whom I could play or hang out.

Fortunately, I met someone in my junior high school who lived on 107th Street between Broadway and Riverside Drive where there were many boys and girls my age. So 107th Street became the hangout spot for me and my new-found friends.

After school we played football games in the street, using sewer covers to mark the goal lines. In the spring and summer we would hang out on the corner with the girls. At this stage in life we seemed to have discovered the opposite sex.

Most of the boys' communications with the girls had to do with teasing and cracking jokes, but we found that we really enjoyed their company. From time to time a girl or boy in the crowd held a birthday party to which the whole crowd was invited.

At these parties we played games that involved kissing, such as "Post Office" and "Spin the Bottle," both of which embarrassed me a great deal, even though I played along. Once I was paired with a pretty girl whom I had to kiss. I gave her a quick peck on the lips and my cheeks turned red. She complained, "You call that a kiss?" I tried to kiss her again, but she would have none of it and walked away in disgust.

With these parties we, and by we I mean the "boys," began to be socialized into the strange world of boy-girl relationships, so that we no longer thought of girls as creatures from another world who should be ignored as we did when we were younger. Soon we learned how to talk with girls, hold hands with them, and even ask them out on dates.

My school pal who introduced me to this scene was named Donald "Lucky" Kramer. How he got the nickname "Lucky" I do not know, but he seemed to be blessed with many qualities that I admired and lacked. He was a good dancer, attractive to girls and very popular. What is more he was one of the few friends I had who lived in his own house, not a rented apartment.

We remained good friends all through junior high school, but when we graduated and went on to different high schools, we lost touch, a cycle that happens again and again with close relationships. I often wonder what we would say to each other if we met again. Would he even remember me as I remember him? Once I wrote a letter to a Donald Kramer whose address I found in a Manhattan phone book, but it must have been another Donald Kramer, for I never received a reply.

As I busied myself with going to school, playing with friends, going to scout meetings, and working during the summers, I approached my thirteenth birthday, a time in the Jewish tradition when I should take part in a ritual known as the Bar Mitzvah, a son of good deeds. Since I left the *Yeshiva* after the death of my grandfather, my only connection to religion was to take my grandmother to temple Saturdays and during the High Holidays of Rosh Hashanah and Yom Kippur.

I received the news that I was to become a Bar Mitzvah with not much enthusiasm, but I knew that I had to prepare for the special ceremony to satisfy my grandmother, who was still quite religious in her own way. Accordingly, a Hebrew teacher was hired to teach me the Hebrew blessings that I had to learn when they called me to the Torah. My teacher was an elderly man with gray hair and glasses who had to supplement his income by preparing boys like me for their Bar Mitzvahs. During my twice-a-week lessons, I tried to race through the Hebrew blessings so as to finish as soon as possible and return to my friends in the street.

The teacher would try to slow me down with the Yiddish words, such as *Hop nichst* (Don't race) which made me slow down a bit, only to resume my hurried pace later on. Somehow I managed to learn enough of the Hebrew to say the necessary blessings when I would be called to the Torah. Several years before, I had attended the Bar Mitzvah ceremony of my cousin, Oscar, who lived in East Orange, New Jersey at the time. Friends and relatives from near and far were invited. I don't remember the actual ceremony, but I do remember that after the ceremony when the family and guests came home, Oscar had received many presents. His young cousins and friends retired to his room and watched with awe as Oscar opened his gifts one by one. There were fountain pens, the kind before ball point pens that had a rubber tube filled with ink. He also received several leather wallets and belts, some gold tie clips, handkerchiefs with his initials, and a good deal of checks and cash.

If I had expected my ceremony to be followed by such munificence, I would have been greatly disappointed. The religious ceremony, in which I did my best not to race through, went smoothly. When the Sabbath services concluded, the congregation was invited to a simple *kiddish* held in another part of the temple. There was the ceremonial blessing for the bread and wine. Then the guests were offered liquor and cake, and that was it. I don't recall receiving any presents aside from the prayer shawl (*talis*) and phylacteries (*tefilin*) which the rabbi gave me on behalf of the congregation.

In those days the fee for my Hebrew teacher, the donation to the temple, and the cost of refreshments was all my family could afford. I know my grandfather would have liked to have seen my Bar Mitzvah, and had he been alive, it would have been a more elaborate celebration.

The last thing I remember about my junior high school was our graduation ceremony. I remember the year 1939 because we wore lapel pins with those numbers inscribed on the pin. For our final assembly we sang a few songs that we had been practicing for almost a year. One was the typical nostalgic song of farewell which used the music from a classic German song and went something like this:

> *Oh, 165, we bid thee fond farewell, how can we bear to part?*
> *Who knows where we may roam, In search of happiness?*
> *Though we may wander far,*
> *Yet school days in dear 165,*
> *We'll never forget,*
> *No, we'll never forget.*

We sang a few more songs, one of which glorified the island country of Cuba, probably because we had a rather large Hispanic population in the school. Then we said good-bye to friends and teachers and went our separate ways.

CHAPTER TWELVE

The role of fate

IN THOSE DAYS WE HAD three choices for high schools. One was Townsend Harris, a high school for the intellectually gifted which required a high average and an entrance exam. Both Laurie Seidman and I took the test; Laurie passed the test and was accepted, but I didn't make it. The other two choices consisted of De Witt Clinton High School, which was for boys only, and George Washington High School, which was co-ed.

I chose to go to George Washington because by this time I was used to girls and enjoyed their company. Our friend from the Boy Scouts, Dick Hyman, chose De Witt Clinton and Kuzy, who had moved away, went to Thomas Jefferson.

Life is like a pinball machine because while we try to direct our lives into certain paths, just as we shoot the steel ball onto the playing field of the pinball machine, the ball as it descends bounces off the pins and goes hither and yon randomly as though it has a mind of its own. If the steel ball represents our destiny, then we have only a modicum of control over its path. We can use "body English" to try to direct the steel ball in a certain direction, but we can apply only so much pressure to influence the descent of the steel ball. Too much pressure on the pin ball machine will cause it to display its "TILT" sign and then the game is over.

All of this is to say that our destiny is decided partly by our own acts and mostly by a series of random events. For example, I made the choice to go to George Washington High School principally because it was the only co-ed high school which was open to me at that time.

At the same time my family decided to move to 150th Street near Riverside Drive. In order to reach the high school on Audubon Avenue and 192nd Street, I had to walk to the 145th Street subway station, which was located on Broadway. I then would take the uptown train to 192nd Street and walk to my high school. Another choice I made was to take a class in French as part of the language requirement for students who might want to continue their education by going to college.

As I mentioned in the Prologue, my French teacher was an avuncular gray-haired teacher whom we called Monsieur Perry. He wore a gray suit with a vest filled with pens.

In a parallel universe there lived a Russian-born girl named Celia Grossman whom I had never met. She lived on 144th Street between Broadway and Amsterdam Avenue and also decided to attend George Washington High School. Her route to school was the same as mine via the subway and, coincidentally, she studied French in the class taught by Monsieur Perry.

Celia sat two rows in front of me in Monsieur Perry's class. I would not have noticed her or paid much attention to this young lady with dark brown eyes and braided, dark brown hair except for the fact that when Monsieur Perry asked a question about France, its language, geography or history, her hand shot up instantly and her answers were invariably correct. I admired her for her wealth of knowledge, but I paid little attention to her. However, random circumstances would change that. For one thing, sometimes purely by chance we met each other on the street going toward the subway station either on the way to or from the school.

On these chance meetings we greeted each other and talked about general topics of interest as we went to and from high school. Another coincidence which brought us together is that she accompanied her grandmother to Saturday services at the Jewish temple on 149th Street near Riverside Drive while I also brought my grandmother to the same temple.

In other words, a random series of circumstances and events brought Celia and me together into a casual friendship, which may have remained that way but for a series of other circumstances which would affect that casual relationship in profound ways which I'll describe later.

I don't remember much about my teachers at George Washington other than Monsieur Perry and a math teacher named Ms. Marx. She was an intense woman with curly blond hair and glasses. She had a strong drive to instill in her students an understanding of the principles of geometry, which soon gave her a reputation among George Washington students as "a good teacher."

Ms. Marx's reputation as a superior teacher became apparent the first day I walked into her classroom. The classroom was designed to hold thirty students, but thirty-six students showed up that first day. When all the seats were filled, the remaining students stood around the sides and the back of the classroom. "Would anyone who has no seat like to go to another math section where there will be room for you?" Ms. Marx asked. Not a soul moved.

"Wouldn't you rather have a seat in another class?" she asked.

"No," said a student. "It's okay. We would rather stand and stay in this class."

I wondered as I sat in Ms. Marx's class that first day what made the teacher so popular? I was soon to find out. I was never good at math, and I had to work hard to keep up with the rest of the students in math classes, but in Ms. Marx's class all that changed.

She presented examples in geometry clearly and carefully. Then she asked questions about the material that she had just presented. If someone failed to answer her question correctly, she stopped and went over the material again until we all understood. Then she gave us some examples to do in class and walked around the room looking at each student's work and helping those who had trouble. For homework she showed us how to fold a standard sized sheet of paper in half, making four surfaces on which we would do four examples similar to those she had taught us that day.

The next time we met, she would return our folded sheets with each example carefully checked and commented on. That means that if Ms. Marx had five classes that met three times a week, she would have gone over 360 examples per week. If someone failed to turn in his or her homework, she knew it right away and asked for a reason the next day that the class met. No matter what the reason, the student had to make up the missing homework so that the next night the student had to do eight examples instead of four.

We soon learned that it did not pay to skip a homework assignment for Ms. Marx's class. At the beginning of the term, Ms. Marx gave her students a kind of survey math test to find out where each student was in terms of math ability.

Apparently, I scored rather low on this survey, so Ms. Marx made me a kind of litmus test for her teaching. Whenever she explained new material, she would look at me. If I looked like I understood the material, she could feel sure that most, if not all, of her students would also have understood what had just been presented. However, if I had a puzzled look on my face, Ms. Marx would go over the material again or give another example to illustrate her point.

With Ms. Marx's careful and clear presentations and her assigned homework examples, I became a good math student, despite my poor prognosis on the math survey. In fact, I began to think that math was an easy subject to learn. Much later on I found out that I was only a good math student because Ms. Marx was such a good teacher.

All in all I think I enjoyed my time at George Washington High School. I did well in languages, French and Spanish, and I enjoyed writing. I became the sports columnist for our school newspaper called *The Cherry Tree*, so named because of the apocryphal story about young George Washington chopping down a cherry tree and owning up to this misdeed because "he could not tell a lie."

I tried out for the baseball team and the track team but didn't make either one. However, thanks to my friend Kuzy, who moved back to Manhattan and transferred from Thomas Jefferson to George Washington in our senior year, I became a member of the handball team.

Kuzy was an excellent handball player, and I was only fair at the game. My friend could not only return any ball that was hit to him, but he had the ability to hit the little black handball so low on the wall that it rolled on the ground after hitting the wall. This shot was called a "killer" because it could not be returned by the opposing players. I, on the other hand, played a good defensive game by returning almost every shot that was hit to my side of the court.

When we played other schools, our opponents figured out that Kuzy was the stronger player, so they tried to keep the ball away from him and played to me. However, since I was able to return most of the shots and Kuzy could cover more than half the handball court, the ball eventually was hit to Kuzy who invariably made his "killer" shot and won the point. As members of the handball team, Kuzy and I received a big letter "W" with a handball court inscribed on the letter. We wore our "letters" on our sweaters and swaggered around like big shots, even though we two were the only members of the handball team.

Chapter Thirteen

The Carnegie Drug Store

LIFE IN HIGH SCHOOL WAS going along smoothly for me: I was a successful student, a writer for the school newspaper, and a letter-wearing member of the handball team. The only fly in the ointment was that I was growing older. I was crossing the line which separated carefree childhood from adolescence.

Up to this point in my life, I did not have any economic obligations toward my Aunt Mamie, who seemed to understand the needs of a teenager and gave me a modest weekly allowance, which took care of my expenses like subway fare, school supplies and an occasional ice-cream soda or sundae. I would have liked this arrangement to continue, but it was not to be.

At this time, my Dad was working at a liquor store on 8th Avenue and 50th Street called Goldberg's. Somehow he learned that the Carnegie Drug Store, located next to Carnegie Hall on 7th Avenue and 57th Street, needed a young man to deliver medicines and such to their customers from six p.m. to midnight on weeknights. My father thought it would be a good idea for me to apply for this job opening.

With mixed feelings I did so and got the job. On the one hand I enjoyed my status as a carefree high school student, but on the other hand, I knew that I had to begin earning some money on my own.

The Carnegie Drug Store was a large drug store in the old-fashioned sense, not the huge supermarket drug store chains of today. It sold drugs and medicines and had a prescription section where prescriptions were made from scratch by a pharmacist who mixed and ground powders with a mortar and pestle. It also had a large soda fountain which extended from the front of the store to the back.

Since the Carnegie Drug Store was ideally located on a busy corner of the city and right next to the famous Carnegie Hall, it was a busy place most of the time, but especially when Carnegie Hall was open with a performance. People going to and from Carnegie Hall would stop in before or after the performance and fill up the seats of the soda fountain, ordering coffee, sandwiches or ice cream treats.

I soon learned that my job in the drug store entailed more than just delivering medicines to customers who phoned in their orders. I was told to clean up the gum wrappers and cigarette butts around the soda fountain where people thoughtlessly dropped them. For this job I had a broom and a metal tray with a long handle which received the sweepings. I was told to do this periodically through the night so that the fountain area floor was kept clean at all times.

I was also told to help the pharmacist when he needed his mortars and pestles to be washed and dried. The pharmacist on night duty was named Steve; he was a large, stocky, elderly man with balding hair. When I was not busy delivering packages or sweeping up the fountain area, I hung out with Steve who befriended me and treated me like his nephew. He would let me mix his creams and powders in his mortars until they were the right consistency, talking to me all the while.

My uniform for this job consisted of a beige jacket with buttons down the front and two pockets on the side. I used the pockets to hold my tips which people were kind enough to give me when I delivered their medicines. I wore the same jacket Monday through Thursday, and on Friday I received a fresh clean jacket.

The Carnegie Drug Store was owned and operated by the Fischer family whose father and two sons took turns working at the store. They worked behind the counters and at the cash register. They were decent bosses, but they saw me as a useful tool to their business, nothing more. Their advice to me was couched in a motto: "Keep busy."

Sometimes when the fountain area was especially busy, I would be asked to join the men at the fountain to wash the dishes, cups and glasses. While performing this chore, I learned about the special language that the fountain men used to call out their orders. For example, an order of coffee was "Draw One," a glass of Coke was "Stretch One," and a malted milk shake was "Burn One," referring to the electric mixer used to make the malted. A bacon, lettuce and tomato sandwich on toast was a "BLT down;" the "down" referred to the act of pushing the toaster lever down to make the toast. "Eight-six" meant that the fountain area had no more of the ordered item.

According to the Morris Dictionary of Word and Phrase Origins, the use of numbers was used by soda fountain men as a kind of code and shorthand for many situations in the fountain area. The soda fountain manager, for instance, was "99," the assistant manager was "98," and a pretty girl in the area was "87 and 1/2." I eventually became a soda fountain worker myself, and used the strange code that only soda fountain workers could understand.

While my job at the Carnegie Drug Store solved my money problem, it created a sleep problem as a side effect. Working until midnight meant that I wouldn't get to sleep until one in the morning. Then I would have to get up at seven in the morning to wash, dress, eat breakfast, and get to school.

While each individual may vary in the amount of sleep he or she needs, my body parts rebelled and told me, "Six hours of sleep won't do; we're going to go on strike and shut you down."

The first three months of my six hours of sleep routine wore me down. I could hardly keep my eyes open. I dragged through the day in a kind of stupor. My sports column for the school newspaper was handed in late, and my school work began to suffer. Instead of focusing on the lessons, I was thinking how nice it would be to lay my head on a soft pillow and sleep. Fortunately my body parts and I reached an accommodation. I learned to take short ten-minute naps during the day like Winston Churchill had done. After school, I would rush home, do my homework and take a ten-minute nap before leaving for work. This compromise with my body's demand for sleep, while not ideal, allowed me to function at school and work.

I probably worked at the Carnegie Drug Store for more than a year. I remember that my battle for enough sleep extended into my first year of college. During the summer months, when I had no classes to attend, I could relax during the day and be ready for work at six p.m. Something happened, however, that changed my summer routine.

A light opera company came to Carnegie Hall and gave matinee performances. That meant that the Carnegie Drug Store became very busy before and after the afternoon performances. The fountain became so busy that the Fischer family decided to clean out part of the basement area and set up tables and chairs to accommodate their overflow customers.

Someone was needed to act as a waiter to take orders and bring food and drinks to these customers. That someone turned out to be me. This meant that almost my entire summer days would be devoted to working at the drug store. I tried to work this way for a week or two, but even though I made more money and received more tips, I was not willing to give up my summer vacation. I summoned up enough courage to tell one of my bosses that I did not want to work extended hours. He became very angry and told me that I was disloyal to the drug store, which only made me more determined to quit. Thereupon I severed my relations with the drug store and did my best to enjoy what was left of my summer vacation.

YOUNG AND OLD

WE ARE NOW LIVING IN the twenty-first century. Young people of today would do well to seek out the elderly to find out what it was like to have lived years ago before we made all that "PROGRESS" and before we "MOVED FORWARD."

Memories of older people could become valuable "antiques" for what my mother-in-law, Sarah, used to call the "younger generation" when she couldn't recall the names of her grandchildren.

For example, when I wanted to demonstrate to my writing students how two people were different from each other, I used the comic strip characters "Mutt and Jeff," Mutt being extremely short, and Jeff being extremely tall. The puzzled look on my students' faces led me to realize that they had no idea what I was talking about. The comic strip had been extinct for many years.

Other examples of how things used to be are Hershey Bars and Baby Ruths which sold for a nickel, which is the same price that a ride on the trolley or subway used to cost. I remember Horn and Hardart Automats where one could get sandwiches, hot food, desserts, coffee and cocoa from a slot machine which accepted only nickels.

I remember that our first radios came with vacuum tubes which had to warm up before we could get a clear signal that produced sound. I remember manual typewriters made by Royal and Remington and fountain pens made by Parker which had to be filled with liquid ink made by a company called Waterman.

However, my favorite memory is about a form of transportation in New York City which was called the double-decker bus. When I gave my notice to the Fischer family that I was quitting my job at the Carnegie Drug Store, I was feeling a bit sad, so I decided to take a bus home instead of the subway.

The bus was run by The 5th Avenue Coach Company and is now part of the city's history, for it is no longer in existence. I am referring to the double-decker green bus that ran on 5th Avenue, Riverside Drive and other routes throughout the city. The bus company employed two men on each bus: the driver; and a man to take the dime fare from each passenger.

Passengers would get on the bus and take a seat. There were no fare boxes on the bus, so a "walking cashier" would appear at the passengers' seats and hold out a kind of metal dime bank into which the passenger would insert a dime which would register on the bank. If the passenger had no dimes, the cash taker would make change and then receive the dime fare in his bank. In the summer the upper deck of the bus was windowless, so the passengers who rode there were exposed to the cool breezes of the summer air.

Riding on the second deck of the bus and watching the scenery as you ride was a much more pleasant ride than the subway. To many, the ten-cent fare of The 5th Avenue Coach Company seemed worth the extra nickel when compared to the subway. Eventually the company went out of business because the buses were no longer cost-effective to run. The double-decker consumed more gas than regular buses, and it had to employ two workers instead of one.

Today, when I see red double-decker buses in Manhattan which are used as tour buses, I miss the ones I used to ride when I had a hard night's work.

In the meantime my senior year was drawing to a close. I went to the prom with a girl whom I met at the Cherry Tree office, and we did the usual things that many high school students do on their prom night. We hired a limo with two other couples and then went to a night club where we had a few drinks at an exorbitant price and then went home.

Before the end of our senior year, however, the guidance counselor helped me fill out my application for college. In my limited financial situation, I had only one choice: The City College of New York which, as I've mentioned before, was free to New York City residents who had a scholastic average of eighty-five or better.

I had managed to attain an eighty-eight average, so I felt I had a chance. Each day after the application was sent in I shuffled through the pile of mail that came to our apartment looking for a letter from City College. For almost a month there was no letter for me. Then one day, the letter did arrive.

With trembling hands I tore open the envelope. As I read the first sentence, my heart started racing. It congratulated me upon being accepted as an undergraduate student at The City College of New York. That was one of the happiest moments of my life. Setting a goal for oneself and then achieving it does wonders for one's self esteem and confidence. I showed my acceptance letter to my family and happily received their congratulations and wishes for success in my new venture.

CHAPTER FOURTEEN

City College

LITTLE DID I KNOW WHAT awaited me when I showed up to register for my freshman year at City College. I was presented with the task of registering for sixteen credits in the courses that were being offered. I had to choose some required courses and some elective courses on days and times that did not conflict, leaving room for some time in which to eat lunch.

The task sounds simple enough, but when you factor in the number of students who are also registering for courses and the fact that each class can hold only a fixed number of students, complications arise. When I finished my scheduling, I was directed to a large room which contained several large blackboards.

On these blackboards were listed the courses and the number of students registered for each. There was a long line of students who had made their schedules and wanted to register. When a student reached the front of the line, an older student, who worked for the registrar, took his schedule and called out his choices to other students who were working the blackboards. The students writing on the blackboard were making hash marks under the course names and sections. This was their way of counting how many students registered for each class. When the hash marks totaled a certain number, like eighteen or twenty, the course and section were closed.

To make the experience of registering even stranger, the student who called out the courses being registered for used the Greek alphabet to designate the sections. He would call out "English 101 Alpha," or "English 101 Beta," or "French 201 Delta."

When it became my turn to register, two of my choices were already closed. I had to go back and refigure my schedule. When I went through the whole process again, I discovered that I had scheduled myself to be in two different classes at the same time, which meant I had to start all over again. Finally, near the end of the day, I had registered for my sixteen credits. I had a severe headache from all the stress, but I was happy to begin my college education.

The expressions "a big fish in a small pond" and "a small fish in a big pond" come to mind as I began my first year at City College. In high school, I was in the top ten percent of my class, but when I got to City College, I found that most of the students were as smart as I was and many more were much smarter. I had to struggle just to keep up.

For example, I enrolled in an advanced algebra class, thinking I could do well in a class that was taught by a dedicated teacher like Ms. Marx, my former high school teacher. But I soon learned that I had no talent for math. The teacher's technique for teaching was to assign a bunch of problems for homework and have students work the examples on the blackboard in class. Your blackboard work was either right or wrong, but no one took the trouble to explain how the right answer was arrived at. The textbook was not much of a help, either. There were many examples to do but the explanations were too brief for me to learn how to do the examples.

I wound up flunking the course and discarding the notion that I could become a civil engineer. My struggle with a history course was not much better. The professor assigned us readings to do in the library and in class he would ask us questions about the readings and mark us on our responses. I tried to do the readings in the library, but since I was still working at the Carnegie Drug Store at night, I only had six hours of sleep, which caused me to fall asleep over my books.

In the entire term in that history class, I didn't get a single answer right whenever my name was called. I just barely passed the course. I did not do much better in biology where I had to dissect a frog. My hands trembled so much that the fellow next to me had to help me peel back the skin of the frog. Again, the teacher asked questions and marked down in his record book whether your answer was right or wrong. I was so tense with this method of instruction that I couldn't even answer correctly when the teacher asked me to state the normal temperature of the human body. I barely passed that course.

While I was floundering in my college courses, world events in Germany and Europe were foreshadowing another conflagration, soon to be named World War II. The German people, impoverished and humiliated by their defeat during World War I, allowed a demagogue, Adolf Hitler, to come to power. The former ne'er-do-well promised to raise the German nation from its defeat and make it a great nation once again.

In order to accomplish this resurgence, Hitler promised to create a powerful army, navy and air force. Since all these plans required a strong central authority he did away with the Weimar Republic and declared himself the dictator of the Third Reich. An important part of Hitler's grandiose scheme to make Germany the greatest nation on earth (*Deutchland uber alles*) was to "purify" the race by getting rid of all those who were not of the Aryan race, principally Jews.

Little did I realize that some egomaniac in Germany would somehow affect my life in America. My life was changed in small, incremental steps.

First, when I turned eighteen, I had to register with the Selective Service System, which meant that I was eligible to be drafted into the armed services. Next, I was cursorily examined by a doctor and placed in the "One A" category, which meant that I would likely be drafted. However, the people at the Selected Service System would allow me to finish out my year in college before I would be drafted.

In the meantime, I had what they euphemistically call "a cash flow problem." Once I quit my job at the Carnegie Drug Store, my pockets became as empty as a politician's promise before an election.

While observing the fountain workers at the drug store while I was washing their glasses and dishes, I determined that the work behind the soda fountain was not too difficult to learn. To make sandwiches from food that was already prepared didn't seem beyond my abilities. Making sodas and ice cream treats also didn't seem to require more than a modicum of skill and training.

So, one day, I presented myself to the union which covered food handlers and soda fountain workers and claimed with more than a little exaggeration, that I was experienced in working behind the soda fountain. I neglected to inform them that my work behind the fountain was confined to dishwashing.

When my interviewer called the Carnegie Drug Store to confirm my claim, I felt that I was doomed, but as luck would have it, there must have been some miscommunication between the union representative and the person who answered the call at the drug store. All I could hear of the conversation was that my interviewer was saying, "Uh-huh, uh-huh, uh-huh."

I thought that when he hung up the phone, he would show me the door, but instead, he asked me to fill out some forms, and I became an official soda fountain man.

My first job was in a "mom and pop" store in Brooklyn. The owner of the store had asked for an experienced counterman who could take care of the fountain for a few hours. When I, this young inexperienced kid, showed up at his store, the owner shook his head in disbelief. I was not what he expected or wanted. However, I was all he had, and until he could get a replacement who was older and more experienced, I would have to do.

So, he gave me an apron and put me behind the soda fountain together with his nephew, who was even younger than I. It took three days for the owner to get a replacement for me, but in those three days I learned a great deal about soda fountain work and could claim to have had "experience."

My next job was with the Whelan Drug Store chain. I was sent to various locations as a substitute worker whenever a regular fountain man called in sick. I remember working at one of their largest stores on 50th Street and 6th Avenue. It was open all night. As one of the fountain men put it, "When they first opened this store, they threw away the key." The experienced fountain men were kind to me, the young, newly experienced kid. They patiently taught me what I needed to know, so that within a short time I knew my way around the fountain and could make a sandwich quickly and efficiently.

Finally I was assigned to a smaller Whelan store on Sundays on a regular basis. I would come in early Sunday morning and open up the soda fountain all by myself. I worked the fountain all day, serving breakfasts, lunches, and sometimes suppers. I also cleaned the dishes and glasses in between serving food and sodas. Sometimes it became so busy that a worker in the drug department had to come behind the fountain area to help me, but most of the time I ran the whole thing alone. I had become a real experienced fountain man, but I had no one to listen to my mastery of the fountain's code like "86" for "we don't have it" or "87 and 1/2" for "look at the pretty girl."

CHAPTER FIFTEEN

Uncle Sam wants you!

AS I KNEW IT WOULD, the letter from the Selective Service System arrived one morning. It began with a strange salutation: "Greetings." It then told me to put "all business aside" and report to active duty.

Early one morning a number of young men, including me, met on a corner near the 145th Street subway station and proceeded to a building near the Whitehall station. We were then loaded on a bus which brought us to the army processing center at Fort Dix, New Jersey, where we were given our shots for various diseases, uniforms for summer and winter, as well as dress uniforms and combat uniforms.

We were also issued metal identifications, which we hung around our necks with a chain and named them "dog tags." All this was done in an assembly-line fashion which would have made the Ford Motor Company envious.

After the war, a TV show featuring Phil Silvers as Sergeant Bilko poked fun at the fast-moving, impersonal nature of the assembly line process by placing a chimpanzee in the assembly line. When the staff who were processing the soldiers on the assembly line asked the chimp a question without looking up from their clipboards, they heard a murmuring sound from the primate. "Speak up," they would bark, still without looking up. So Sergeant Bilko and his buddies named the chimp, "Harry Speak-Up." The TV show reached its climax when the army learned that it had inducted a chimpanzee, named "Harry Speak-Up," into its ranks.

However, the real-life situation that first day was no laughing matter. The shots were painful and the amount of stuff that was thrust at us was overwhelming.

At the Fort Dix Processing Center we were indoctrinated into the army way of doing things. The saying among the new recruits was that there were three ways of doing things: the right way, the wrong way, and the army way. We learned how to shine our shoes so that we could almost see our faces in them; how to make a bed with hospital corners and the blanket so tight that a coin tossed on the bed would bounce. We learned how to clean our barracks so that not a speck of dust remained anywhere, and we also learned how to endure an entire day in the kitchen, setting tables, waiting tables, busing tables, and cleaning a mountain of dishes, pots and pans for an entire company of men.

Taking part in these procedures was designated as being part of the "Kitchen Police" or KP for short. My first experience with KP taught me something much more fundamental than how to wash dishes, pots, and pans. It all began when the loud speaker system began with, "Now hear this. The following men will report for kitchen duty at 0600 hours. Altman, Brodsky, Cohen, Chen, Finkelstein, Goldberg, Hoffman, etc." All I noticed about the list of names was that I was on it.

An older and more perceptive soldier, however, noticed something more about the list for KP. All the names on the list, except Chen, who was Chinese, were Jewish. The soldier, who was also Jewish and on the KP list pointed out the selective nature of the KP list to the sergeant in charge. The sergeant thereupon summoned the corporal who was from a southern state, possibly Georgia.

"Did you deliberately choose all Jewish names for your KP list?" the sergeant asked.

The corporal's face turned bright red as he admitted, "Yeah, I hate the Jews," he said with no trace of remorse.

Whereupon the sergeant tore up the list and got someone else to draw up a new KP roster. As luck would have it, I was also on the new list that was announced over the loud speaker system. This was really my first encounter with anti-Semitism. I had heard about it in news broadcasts and in the ravings of people like Father Coughlin, but this blind racial hatred had never touched me personally until that day in the army when a corporal used his rank and authority to express his hatred toward people he didn't even know.

I don't remember much about the day I spent on KP except that it began early the morning when the cook awakened me. He was assembling his crew and went from bed to bed awakening people who were on his list. It must have been five o'clock in the morning when all of us on KP assembled in the mess hall to prepare for breakfast. I remember helping to set the many long tables for breakfast.

We set out the plates, glasses, and silverware and coffee cups for more than 1,000 soldiers. What struck me as particularly odd was the way we were told to align the coffee cups. All the handles had to be positioned in the same direction, and we had to take a very long piece of string from one end of the mess hall to the other. One soldier held the string at the back of the mess hall, and another soldier held his end at the front. The string was used to center the cups on the table so that they formed a straight line at the center of the tightly held string. Why they bothered to align the cups like soldiers on a parade ground, when they would be dispersed as soon as the soldiers sat down was a question whose answer was known only to the army.

When the hungry soldiers came in and formed a chow line, we who were on KP served them, cafeteria style, with eggs, juice, bacon, cereal and toast. The eggs were usually scrambled and kept in large metal tubs, almost as big as garbage cans. After a few minutes, they became cold and tasted like rubber.

At breakfast's end, we had to bus the tables, wash the dishes, pots, pans, and silverware; then we had to reset the tables for lunch. The process was the same as breakfast, except the menu was different.

Keeping dishes and silverware clean and free of grease was a big concern of the army and especially the chief cook, for cooking and cleaning for so many men might invite the spread of dysentery if the dishes and utensils were not thoroughly clean.

Therefore, we had to scrub the dishes clean in extremely hot soapy water and then rinse them in boiling hot water. The water was so hot that we could not touch the dishes with our bare hands. We had to lift the dishes with a large spatula placed under the dishes to transfer them from the soapy sink to the rinsing sink.

When the dishes were dry, the cook would test them for cleanliness with his thumb. Dishes which were thoroughly clean and free from grease would make a squeaky sound. Perhaps that thumb inspection gave rise to the phrase, "squeaky clean." On the other hand, dishes which had a slight trace of grease would make no sound. Those dishes had to be rewashed and re-dried.

Our barracks were plain, two-story frame buildings with bunk beds aligned along each side of the wall. On the first Saturday that we were at Fort Dix, a sergeant informed us that our building was to be inspected. That meant that all traces of dust and dirt had to be removed by washing, scrubbing and mopping. Even the windows and screens had to be washed. We worked all morning with buckets of soapy water, mops, brooms and cleaning rags to make our poor barracks as clean as possible. When we were finished a lieutenant came by wearing white gloves. He rubbed his gloved hand on the window sills and other places known for collecting dust, but his white gloves remained unsoiled, so we passed inspection.

During our time off at the reception center, we could go to the Post Exchange or PX to buy beer, cigarettes and toilet articles. There was a juke box in the PX, which produced a loud booming sound when a coin was deposited. Mostly it played "The Beer Barrel Polka." The beer we were permitted to buy was a weakened version of real beer; it contained only 3.2% alcohol, and it tasted flat when compared to real beer, but it smelled like beer, so we drank it and pretended it tasted good.

I don't remember how long we stayed at Fort Dix, but soon a number of us were shipped out for our thirteen weeks of basic training to Camp Shelby, Mississippi. We rode the train for three days and nights.

Some of the soldiers passed the time by playing poker, and some just sat around and talked. I spent a lot of time just gazing out of the window at the passing scenery.

Camp Shelby is located in southern Mississippi, closer to Alabama on the east than to Louisiana on the west. Its climate is hot and moist during the summer and fairly cold in the winter. The nearest town to Camp Shelby is Hattiesburg, a little hospitable town that held dances for the soldiers when they got a pass to town.

Soon after our arrival at Camp Shelby, we were informed that we had to go to the base barber shop to get a GI (Government Issue) haircut which was a short, short haircut, leaving us almost bald. The reason given for insisting on this scalping was that in the case of hand-to-hand combat, the enemy would have no opportunity to grab a soldier by his hair. Another reason given was that since soldiers would be spending a great deal of time in the field, there would be no time to shampoo a full head of hair, and unwashed hair could lead to all kinds of health problems, including head lice.

At any rate, we were not *asked* to get short haircuts; we were *told* to. When the barber was finished running his electric clipper over my scalp, I was not only almost bald, but I had another problem: my head was smaller than the army had planned for, so that my helmet liner, a plastic liner worn under the steel helmet, was too large for my little head. During close-order drill when we were marching up and down the field, turning right and left on command, my head spun inside my helmet when I made a right or left turn. This left me in an awkward position because while my body made a right turn, my helmet remained ninety degrees to the left.

I finally learned how to compensate for my loose helmet by placing my hand on top of my head whenever I had to turn so that my body and helmet made the right or left turn together as a unit. Had I been able to keep a full head of hair, this problem might have been avoided.

Our living quarters were Spartan with about sixteen soldiers assigned to each one-story, white wooden barracks. There were two pot belly stoves in each barracks, a clue to the severely cold winters that plagued Camp Shelby.

Although we trained together for thirteen weeks, I scarcely remember any of my bunk mates. There was one recently married soldier who could not stand being separated from his young bride. Eventually he became so distraught that he attempted to dismantle the pot belly stove in our barracks and throw it out the door. He was taken to the hospital and later discharged from the army.

There was also a fellow who, despite his diminutive size, was promoted to a corporal during basic training because he caught on so quickly to everything that was being taught from how to disassemble and reassemble a rifle to how to dig a foxhole.

There was also a guy from Mississippi who hated New Yorkers and boasted how Mississippi was superior to that eastern city in every way. We had some interesting conversations until I realized that his mind was set and he would not change it, no matter how much I argued with him.

Then there was a soldier from Armenia, with whom I shared a tent whenever we went on maneuvers in the field. His name I remember; it was Dakak, and we got along well together. Also there was a fellow who played the clarinet, who eventually got a job playing in the company band; and a fellow from the south who kept calling me "Corn" instead of Cohen. He continually borrowed money from me to go into town and get drunk.

Our company was led by a man named Captain Leonard, who in civilian life had been some kind of salesman. He was a short man with a trim muscular body and short-cropped, steel gray hair. He was a bit on the "gung-ho" side, always wanting L Company to be the best in the whole regiment.

I lost my respect for Captain Leonard for the way he handled the problem of a soldier who had a weak bladder and wet his bed each night. Captain Leonard made the soldier sleep outside under the mess hall as punishment for wetting his bed instead of recognizing that the soldier had a medical problem.

Chapter Sixteen

Basic training

IT WAS THE ARMY'S PLAN to take raw recruits and turn them into soldiers in thirteen weeks, a formidable task. To accomplish this we were issued a rifle, an M-1 Garand, and taught how to keep the rifle clean, especially the bore of the rifle, for even a speck of sand in the rifle bore could affect the accuracy of the bullet when the rifle was fired.

Every evening, after we had returned from training in the field, and after we had showered and shaved, we assembled for inspection. A second lieutenant would bark out a command to "Present Arms!" This command called for each soldier to bring up his rifle to his chest at a forty-five degree angle with the barrel pointing upward past the left shoulder.

When the lieutenant stood in front of a soldier, that soldier sharply handed his rifle to the lieutenant, who looked down the barrel to see that it was free of dirt. Then the lieutenant would hand the rifle back to the soldier, who would pull the trigger to show that the rifle was not loaded, and then place the rifle at his side with the butt resting on the ground. Once, when I pulled the trigger during this inspection process, the rifle made a loud bang because I had neglected to remove a blank bullet from the rifle's chamber. The inspecting lieutenant was not happy when he heard that loud explosion, but since it was only a blank that went off, he gave me a warning about inspecting the rifle's chamber before inspection.

Not only were our rifles inspected daily, but our personal grooming was also checked. That meant, among other things, that our faces had to be clean shaven.

Another time, after a hard day in the field, I was too tired to shave. When the company commander, Captain Leonard, approached me during inspection he asked, "Have you shaved today, soldier?"

"Yes, Sir," I lied, trying to avoid another stain on my inspection record.

"Well, next time, stand a little closer to the razor," the Captain barked and moved on to the next soldier.

There came a time when we soldiers not only had to learn how to disassemble and reassemble our Garand rifles, but we had to learn how to shoot them as well.

To accomplish this task, we had to spend several days in the field near the rifle range. Spending days in the field and sleeping in our tents was called a bivouac. That meant that each soldier had to pair off with another soldier in order to erect a tent since each soldier carried in his backpack only half a tent, called a shelter half, and a tent pole and pegs.

I teamed up with the young Armenian named Dakak. First we buttoned the two shelter halves together to form a large rectangle. Then we inserted tent poles into the tent grommets. Next we made the tent taut with rope and tent pegs. We drove the tent pegs deep into the ground with our folding trench shovels, which doubled as hammers. Then we dug a little trench around the perimeter of the tents so that rain water would be channeled sway from our tent in case it rained. If we were camped near pine trees, we would place their branches on the ground inside our tent to make a kind of soft mattress.

Dakak and I could set up our tent in about five minutes, once we got the hang of the operation. It was amazing how we learned to sleep so comfortably in these primitive pup-tents.

Many years later after the war, my wife, Celia, and I together with our friends, Lenore and Charley Becker, used to go camping during our summer vacations. We often went to a state park in Vermont, where we enjoyed a week's vacation sleeping in tents which were larger and more comfortable than army pup-tents, but the basic principle was the same.

The main purpose for this particular bivouac was to learn how to shoot accurately with our rifles. First they taught us how to pull

LAWRENCE H. COHEN

our triggers without any bullets in the chamber from various positions, i.e., standing, sitting, and prone, so we would learn how to hold our rifles as still as possible as we pulled our triggers. After a day of pretend firing we were given real bullets and taken to the firing range. When real bullets are involved, safety procedures become very important.

During basic training, I witnessed a shooting accident in which one member of the Military Police shot another MP by accident at close range. "I didn't know the gun was loaded!" shouted the shooter as his buddy writhed in pain from the bullet wound in his abdomen.

In order not to have stray bullets going off at the wrong time, the rifle range officer would shout the following before we would shoot at the targets: "Ready on the right; ready on the left; ready on the firing line; ready, aim, fire!" Then those on the firing line began shooting at a large target, perhaps 200 yards away. The target was a large bullseye with a tiny black center and larger concentric circles around the bullseye.

The goal of the shooter was to shoot as many bullseyes as possible or, failing that, to hit the circles nearest to the bullseye. At last my turn came to lie down on the firing line and shoot at the target. The Garand rifle held a clip of ten bullets, so I would be allowed to fire ten bullets a time. After everyone on the firing line had shot his ten bullets, the firing line officer would shout, "Cease Fire!"

Then the targets would be pulled down and graded by soldiers working in the target pits. They would count the number of "hits" in the bullseye and in the surrounding circles. Then they would hold up number signs for each target like the judges in Olympic events. If the soldier failed to hit any part of the target, they would wave a red flag, indicating a zero score. The red flag score was called a "Bolo." The derivation of "Bolo" is unclear but its meaning left no doubt that the shooter was "disgraceful" and needed more training.

Having never fired a rifle in my life, except for a "bee-bee" gun, I was unprepared for the loud explosive bang and the tremendous "kick" of the rifle as my first shot rang out. My body's natural reaction to the loud noise was to flinch. The flinch caused the rifle to move off target so that my first shot was nowhere near the bullseye. Each time I pulled the trigger, I automatically flinched, and each time I flinched, I missed the target completely. Out of ten shots, I hit the target not once, and so my score was a red flag. I was a "Bolo."

After the order for "Cease Fire," the targets were repaired by placing a sticker over the bullet holes, so that the next shooter could start with a target that had no bullet holes. During this lull on the firing range, officers and NCO's came over to help the poor shooters like me. A mild-mannered lieutenant colonel came over to help me. He told me to squeeze the trigger slowly and not to flinch at the loud explosion of the gun powder.

"Easier said than done," I thought to myself. The colonel then told me to close my eyes while he inserted a single bullet in my rifle's chamber. "Now squeeze the trigger and don't flinch," he said. I did so and heard a gentle click. The colonel had inserted a blank in my rifle. I had not flinched.

Then, while my eyes were closed, he inserted another bullet. I squeezed the trigger and heard a loud bang. Once again I flinched. The colonel used his strategy again and again, interspersing blanks with real bullets, but I flinched every time the real bullet was fired. The colonel sighed as he left me indicating that I was hopeless when it came to firing a rifle at a target.

I was given two more chances to fire my rifle at the target, but I flinched each time I fired, missing the target for each of my twenty shots and seeing the red flag each time my score was tallied. I was a "Bolo" and a disgrace to Company L. Captain Leonard washed his hands of me and handed me over to a first lieutenant who happened to be Jewish.

Lieutenant Lewis was young and tall. He was also mild mannered like the colonel who had tried to help me on the firing line. The young lieutenant reminded me of the Boy Scout leaders who ran our scout troop when I was young. We left the firing range and went back to our campsite where Lieutenant Lewis took me aside and explained why he was assigned by Captain Leonard to help me with my marksmanship, or lack of it. "He thinks that because I'm Jewish, I can relate to you better than he can," he said.

"It's not about being Jewish," I said. "I've never touched a rifle in my life, and when I hear a loud noise, I jump. I just can't help it."

"I know," said the lieutenant," but if you concentrate on not flinching, you can overcome this tendency to jump when the rifle is fired. Try to say to yourself that you know there's going to be a loud noise when you fire the rifle. Since you expect the noise, you can prepare your brain not to flinch when the rifle makes its noise." With that he had me pull the trigger on my unloaded rifle again and again. Each time I pulled the trigger, I said to myself, "Don't flinch."

For the next two days I followed the lieutenant's instruction faithfully. I practiced firing in all the positions that we were taught, standing, sitting and prone. I told myself that when real bullets are used, I can expect to hear a loud explosion, and since it is expected, I needn't fear it. I should hold the rifle steady and not flinch. Two days later, I went back to the firing range. When my turn came to go on the firing line, I heard the range officer give his commands in a loud drawn-out voice: "Ready on the right! Ready on the left! Ready on the firing line!

"Ready! Aim! Fire!" I squeezed off my first shot. The explosive force that gave life to the bullet's flight made its usual bang, but I was prepared for it and did not react.

Calmly and deliberately, I shot all ten bullets at the target, brushing aside the noise from the explosions. My target was pulled down and graded. This time there was no red flag. Instead they raised a sign indicating a high score. I scored well from all shooting positions, including a rapid fire exercise in which I had to shoot the first bullet, then remove a clip from my belt pouch, insert it into the rifle and fire as rapidly as I could at the target.

From all these positions, I earned a very high score; so high was my score that I was designated a "sharpshooter." I had traveled the road from a "Bolo," who couldn't hit the side of a barn with his rifle to a "sharpshooter," thanks to the calming words of Lieutenant Lewis and my determination to master the skill of shooting a rifle. For the first time in my army life, I was proud of myself.

After conquering my fear of loud noises from rifle shooting, I was confronted with another problem that was not so easy to solve. It happened while I was on guard duty. The army manual for guard duty states that a soldier on guard duty should "...walk [his] post in a military manner."

I can't remember the rest of the instructions except that when a guard hears someone approaching his area, he is supposed to shout: "HALT! WHO GOES THERE? ADVANCE AND BE RECOGNIZED."

Of course, in basic training, the only one who would be approaching a guard at night would be an officer who is checking to see that the guard is "walking his post in a military manner" and is not asleep. Nevertheless, the guard is supposed to challenge the inspecting officer as though he were a stranger. Walking a post "in a military manner" means that the guard is marching a specified area with his rifle resting over his right shoulder with its butt held in the palm of his right hand.

One night I pulled guard duty and was walking my post when I began to sense that all was not well with my health. First, I had to throw up and then I had a bad case of diarrhea. Next I noted that my head ached, not just a simple headache but a severe pain in my frontal lobe, the most severe pain I have ever experienced.

When the inspecting officer came around to check on me, I told him about my severe headache. The company medic was called, and he took my temperature, which turned out to be a very high fever. In normal circumstances, an ambulance would be called, and I would have been rushed to the base hospital.

However, as luck would have it, the ambulances were out on a field exercise and none were available that night. The officers brought me extra blankets, and gave me aspirin, which did not help at all. The next morning, an ambulance did finally arrive and transported me to the base hospital where it took the doctors about a day to figure out what was wrong with me.

After administering a spinal tap, they finally determined that I had spinal meningitis, which is an inflammation of the membranes covering the brain and spinal cord. In the early 1940's, the drug used to fight spinal meningitis was sulfur. It probably saved my life. I was given a daily dose of the drug, but the doctors had to make sure that the drug did not harm my kidneys, so they had me drink a lot of water, one eight ounce glass every four hours around the clock.

At night while I was sleeping, an orderly would wake me and hand me my glass of water. At first I had to keep my head flat against the mattress, so I could not use a pillow. However, after three days, I was given a pillow and by this time my headache was gone.

One day, while I was still in the hospital, a chaplain came to see me. He informed me that I almost had succumbed to the infection, and he was glad to see that I made it. I stayed in the hospital recuperating for about three weeks, and then I was released and sent back to my company where I resumed basic training.

One of the most anticipated events in basic training is "Mail Call." That is when the company clerk calls out, "MAIL CALL." He doesn't have to say it twice, for immediately the soldiers drop everything to assemble around the company clerk who calls out the last name of soldiers and hands them letters and packages from home. Letters from home are the closest thing to connecting with family and friends, and they are invaluable in keeping up the morale of soldiers who are away from home in a place they don't want to be and doing things that they don't like to do.

As far as receiving these valuable letters from home, I was fairly lucky. My steadiest and most frequent letter writer was Celia Grossman, my friend from high school. She wrote to me almost twice a week and sent me homemade cookies, which made me and my bunkmates happy. Her letters were newsy, about what was going on at home and always ended with S W A C K (Sealed With

A Kiss).Of course I replied to her letters and we kept up our correspondence all through the war. Celia's letters and cookies convinced me that we would be together after the war.

My Dad didn't write long letters, but he sent me "care packages" consisting of salamis from the local delicatessen. The soldiers in my barracks were happy when the salamis were passed around. My best friend, Laurie Seidman, was a frequent writer whose sense of humor sparkled in his letters and cheered me up a great deal.

CHAPTER SEVENTEEN

Overseas

ONE DAY NEAR THE END of our basic training, we were informed that we would be going overseas. Before that happened, we were given two weeks' leave to return to our family. At first, two weeks sounded like a long time, but it took three days by train to reach New York and three days to return to Mississippi, so that left only about a week to visit family and friends. I certainly enjoyed my leave, but the fact that I was going overseas hung like a dark cloud over me and my family and friends.

I returned to Camp Shelby and prepared for my trip to God-Knows-Where. The night before we were to depart, they gave us a steak dinner with all the beer we could drink. The meal was a pleasant break from the usual army fare, but it felt like the last meal of a prisoner on death row.

The next day, word came down that we would be "shipping out" the following day. We were told to pack two barracks bags, an "A" bag, which we would keep with us and a "B" bag, which would go aboard our ship but would no longer be our property. The "B" bag would be replacement clothing for other soldiers who were overseas. We were told which kind of clothing would go into each of the bags.

In short, one bag was for us to keep with us while we were on the front lines. Soon we were put on a train bound for a port city which I had never learned about in my geography class. It was called Newport News, Virginia.

It took us several days to get there and when we arrived we boarded what was called a "Liberty Ship," a euphemism for a ship packed from top to bottom with its cargo of soldiers. To save space we slept in hammocks suspended from poles. Not only was the hold of the ship crowded, but it wreaked of cigarette smoke.

As we zigzagged across the Atlantic in order to avoid the German U-Boats which lurked deep in the ocean, the ship rolled unmercifully from side to side. The roll of the ship did not bother the crew or most of the soldiers, but it gave me the worst case of seasickness I have ever known. I was confined to my hammock for the entire journey of seven days.

I left my hammock only to go to the bathroom or "head," as the sailors called it. Trying to wash my hands with soap in the "head" taught me that soap will not make a lather in salt water, which was the only kind of water used for washing up after using the bathroom. Even aboard ship there was KP for the enlisted men.

When a crew member approached me as I lay in my hammock, he noticed my almost green complexion and kindly excused me from this chore. Other soldiers, who were not so overcome by the rolling ship, went up on deck and played poker or walked around the ship.

Finally we landed in Oran, a seaport in Algeria, North Africa on the Mediterranean Sea. I don't remember much about our encampment in Oran except that I caught the worst case of diarrhea in my life. I should have remembered the lessons that the cooks in Camp Shelby had taught me about the need for squeaky clean utensils to avoid catching a case of this dreaded disease. After eating our meals from our mess kits, we were told to line up in front of two large cans, one filled with soapy water and the other filled with boiling hot rinse water. We would wash out our mess kits with a brush in the soapy water and then rinse them off in the rinse water. One day I found myself at the end of the line for washing out our mess kits. By the time I reached the front of the line, the washing water and the rinse water were no longer as clean or as hot as they were at the beginning. Apparently my mess kit did not get washed as thoroughly as it should have, which may account for my coming down with a bad case of diarrhea.

While in Oran, I was assigned to the Third Army. I was placed with a group of soldiers who had been in the Italian campaign. These were soldiers who had forged common bonds with each other. They regarded me as an unnecessary intruder and for the most part they ignored me. In North Africa our training consisted mostly of practicing for a landing in southern France.

We would board boats called Landing Craft Infantry (LCI's). The small motor boat could hold up to twenty men and could move swiftly in the water. The front end of the boat could be lowered to form a ramp enabling the soldiers to debark swiftly. We practiced boarding and landing almost every day until the procedure became routine.

When we were not practicing landing with the LCI's, we practiced marching up and down the camp; it was called "close order drill." The drill sergeant would count the cadence to keep the soldiers in step with one another. He would call out, "Hup, two, three, four. Hup, two, three, four." Then he might command, "By the left flank, march!" Each soldier would then execute a left turn and continue marching. The sergeant might also call out, "Column, left, march!" in which case the soldiers on the left of the squad would turn left and the others to his right would follow him until the entire squad had done a 90 degree turn to the left.

The drill sergeant had to be skilled in keeping the cadence so that the marching soldiers remained in step with one another, no matter what the command. One day the drill sergeant decided to let some of the enlisted men take turns in drilling the marching men. Each soldier got a turn to call out the cadence and the various marching commands.

It was then that we learned that acting as a drill sergeant was not as easy as it seemed. First of all, the commands consisted of two parts: a preparatory part like "Column left" or "Column right," and the execution part, "March!" The word "March!" had to be given just before the left or right foot struck the ground. If the command involved a right turn, then the word "March" had to be called just before the right foot would strike the ground, and if the command involved a turn to the left, then "March!" had to be called just before the left foot would strike the ground.

One day the drill sergeant called on a soldier to call out the commands for our close order drill. The soldier who acted as drill sergeant didn't realize that the command had to be called at a specific time. As a result the marching soldiers got out of step and the marching had to be halted. The soldier who was drilling our squad had to return to the ranks. He was quite upset and embarrassed.

Then the drill sergeant called on me to drill the squad. For some strange reason, I had practiced marching and calling out the commands on the correct foot, and so I did pretty well as a substitute drill sergeant. Little did I know that the soldier who had preceded me and who did not fare so well as a drill sergeant would resent my success following his failure.

After our close order drill, we returned to our tent to await the call to lunch which we called "Chow Call." My spot in the eight-man tent was near the tent entrance on the right-hand side. Opposite me was the pad of the soldier who messed up as a drill sergeant.

I noticed that he was fiddling around with a hand grenade, but I didn't pay much attention to what he was doing with that grenade. All of a sudden he rolled the grenade toward me. It seemed to be a "live" grenade and the fuse made a hissing sound. All the soldiers in the tent bolted out of the tent as fast as they could get to their feet and run. The one who had rolled the grenade at me was the first one out. I could do nothing but cower in my corner of the tent and shield my face from the anticipated explosion.

In a flash I recalled the training we had received about the use of hand grenades. Our practice sessions with live grenades consisted of lobbing grenades into a large deep dirt pit where the explosions would do no harm to humans. Since no one had paid attention to the soldier who was working with the grenade, we all thought that he had rolled a live grenade in our tent. We were unaware that the soldier who was fiddling with the grenade had removed all of the explosive powder, leaving just the fuse. He then pulled the pin, released the metal safety spring, and rolled the powder-less grenade toward me.

As I cowered on the ground after everyone had sprung out of the tent, I expected to hear the same kind of explosion that I heard when I practiced throwing grenades into an earthen pit. Instead I heard the hissing sound of the fuse and then silence, dead silence.

The soldier who had fixed the powderless grenade reentered the tent with a satisfied smile on his face as he looked at my curled-up body. The other men realized what had happened and returned relieved to their tent, but they let the perpetrator know that they didn't regard his action as a harmless prank; they resented being scared to death by one of their own, and they told him so in no uncertain terms.

As for me, I recognized that his so-called joke was really a deep-seated hatred for me, not only because of the close order marching incident, but probably due to his anti-Semitism. Although we were never friends before this incident, we became even more distant after. So far in my army career, I experienced two forms of anti-Semitism: one when a corporal assigned me to KP simply because I was Jewish and the other when a soldier expressed his hatred by rolling a powder-less grenade in my direction.

In contrast to this frightening experience, there were some pleasant happenings that came my way. One of these occurred when my good friend, Laurie Seidman, discovered that our two army units were near one another. He managed to find my unit and paid me a visit. Laurie had become a medic whose job it was to treat wounded soldiers in the field before they were transferred to a hospital or a M.A.S.H. unit, a kind of mobile surgical hospital.

He probably called upon his Boy Scout training of using his bandana to improvise bandages for various types of wounds in his new army job. At any rate we were glad to see each other and share the news about our respective lives. While visiting, Laurie showed me a very funny letter written by our friend Milton (Kuzy). He had written this long letter on toilet paper and sent it to Laurie. Kuzy had wound up in the army as a baker, so the three former Boy Scouts had become a medic, a baker and a rifleman in the United States Army.

Chapter Eighteen

Second invasion: Southern France

THE ORDERS CAME DOWN ONE day to strike our tents and pack our gear because we were shipping out. We were to march to a huge staging area where we would be loaded onto trucks which would take us to the port of Oran again. In all of the excitement of packing, I forgot to bring my rifle along. I left it standing against a tent pole. Imagine my embarrassment when we reached our staging area and discovered that I was a rifleman without a rifle. Without saying a word to anyone, I ran back to where our tent had been.

Fortunately they had not gotten around to striking our tent, and the rifle was standing right where I had left it. I seized the rifle and ran back to our staging area, but our company had already boarded their trucks and they were rolling toward the port. Luckily there were hundreds of trucks going in the same direction, so I hitched a ride in one of them and eventually found my unit. No one had even missed me. I felt as though no one cared whether I was part of the unit or not; I was on the outside looking for a seat at the table, like the player who failed to find a chair in the game of "Musical Chairs."

While waiting to board our ship, I wondered what Freud would have said about a rifleman who forgets to take his rifle to an impending assault on the enemy? My memory about how we navigated from Oran is hazy. I do remember reaching Naples. From there we headed for Marseille in southern France. On the last leg of our journey, we boarded the LCI's on which we had practiced landing for so many days, but this journey was not practice; it was the real thing.

It was quiet aboard the LCI where all the soldiers were standing. We knew that the Normandy landing in northern France had not gone so smoothly and there had been many casualties as the men poured out of their landing craft and onto the shore. Would this landing also be met with German machine gun and mortar fire? We had no way of knowing, but just before the boat came near the shore and the ramp was lowered, I saw a number of soldiers make the sign of the cross as they prepared to run ashore.

I envied them for the faith they had in making the gesture, as though the sign of the cross would somehow protect them from harm. Such faith and comfort was denied me, for the closest thing the Jewish religion has to the cross symbol is the Star of David, two inverted interlocking equilateral triangles, which cannot be signed across the chest in time to prevent an impending disaster. I had to leave the boat without any message to the Powers That Be, but I did stay close behind a soldier who had made the sign of the cross, hoping any protection that he had would also shield me.

Fortunately, our boat and all the other boats that made that landing in August 1944 did not come under fire. In fact the German army in southern France was in retreat so the Third Army advance did not meet resistance. We advanced from Marseille to the beautiful city of Lyon with its broad, tree-lined avenues.

The French people greeted us enthusiastically as heroes and their children gathered around us to receive gifts of chewing gum and chocolate bars. As we stopped for lunch, which consisted of a can of beans and vegetables which could be heated over a campfire, a piece of cheddar cheese, some crackers and some powdered coffee, some French people brought us red wine and some onions to make our can of beans more palatable. Sometimes we marched north to the next town and sometimes we boarded trucks to chase the retreating army.

From Lyon we approached a fairly large town northeast of Lyon called Besancon (pronounced bay-zan-SON), which is large enough to have a dot next to its name on the map of France. As we approached Besancon, our company was given the assignment to secure a bridge near the town. We assumed that there was no danger involved in this mission since we had heard for several days that the German army was in retreat. Therefore, we walked down the middle of a paved road with the moonlight as our guide.

Since I knew how to speak a little French from my high school days, I was positioned at the head of the column in case I had to ask a villager about the whereabouts of the Germans. (*"Ou est les Alemands?"* Where are the Germans? *"Ou est le pont?"* Where is the bridge?) Soon our foot soldiers were joined by a tank, which gave us even more confidence that our mission would soon be accomplished.

All of a sudden our peaceful walk in the moonlight was shattered by a burst of fire from several machine guns called "burp guns" because the fire resembled the sound "brrrp." Every man in the column threw his body to the ground and then scrambled to the side of the road, including me.

As I was crawling to the side of the road, I felt a sharp pain in my left leg, just below the knee and another in my left toe, the digit immediate to the left of my big toe. (In the rhyming game called "This Little Piggy Went to Market" the pain came from the "little piggy {that} stayed home.")

While our platoon was cowering in the road, our great big tank was just sitting in the middle of the road. One of our second lieutenants, a lot braver than most, was pounding on the hatch of the tank with his baton, trying to get the tank crew to engage in battle with the Germans who were shooting at us with their burp guns. The tank crew, however, refused to do anything except close their hatch and remain motionless. They refused to join in the battle. In about five minutes the shooting stopped and we heard the Germans leave the area in motorcycles and jeeps.

We learned later that this was a German rear-guard action, designed to slow down the pursuing Third Army so that the retreating German Army would have a better chance of escaping. When the shooting stopped and the German soldiers left in their vehicles, the medics came to treat a few wounded soldiers. A medic came to me and cleaned my two wounds. He then poured sulfur powder on the wounds and bandaged them. A French villager appeared with a shot of cognac, which he signaled me to gulp down;

I did so and began to feel warm inside.

In this brief encounter, the only one I was to experience during the entire war, I had received one grazing wound that went through my skin just below the knee and a wounded toe. In the military, wounds of this sort are called "million dollar wounds" because while they are not permanently incapacitating, they are severe enough to send the wounded soldiers to the hospital in the "zone of the interior" (ZI).

I was taken by ambulance to a mobile hospital which consisted of a large tent erected behind the front lines, a M.A.S.H. unit. There the surgeons gave me a general anesthetic and removed the bullet from my toe. When I awoke, they handed me the bullet fragment in a tiny vial as a keepsake. When I was well enough to be moved, they evacuated me by airplane to a make-shift hospital in Naples where I recuperated for a month or so.

The hospital itself consisted of a very large room, probably made up from someone's former palace. There were about ten beds on each side of the large room and a nurse's station in the corner. Most of the patients were recuperating from surgery on their wounds, just like I was. I remember a Hawaiian sergeant in the bed opposite mine who had a box of candy bars which he passed around to the soldiers in the beds near his.

My wounds were healing nicely when one day a major came around to each bed and examined the wounds on each soldier. His mission was to clear up some hospital beds by sending soldiers whose wounds had healed sufficiently back to their outfits. Fortunately for me, my wounds, though on the mend, were not completely healed. The major ordered that I be examined again in a week. Luck was with me again later when the week was up and a Jewish captain examined my wounds. He said, "Your wounds are almost healed. I can send you back to your outfit in a few days or I can send you back behind the lines for non-combative duty. Which do you want me to do?"

I couldn't believe my ears. Here was this doctor giving me a choice: back to the front, or non-combat duty in the zone of the interior. I did not agonize over the decision for a second. I had not formed any close relationships with the men in my outfit. I had been a replacement who was not needed in the outfit. In fact, one of the soldiers in my unit had tried to frighten me by rolling a powderless grenade at me. So I chose to be sent to the back of the lines for limited duty. That Jewish doctor may have saved my life, for the Germans, though retreating, were not through fighting yet. They were preparing for one last effort to turn the war around by breaking out of the trap set by the surrounding Allied forces. That last effort was called the Battle of the Bulge, a fierce battle with many casualties on both sides.

Before I left the hospital for my new assignment, a Warrant Officer came around to my bed and awarded me the "Purple Heart," a medal for wounded soldiers that dates back to George Washington and his Continental Army.

The Purple Heart medal consists of three parts: a rectangular bar pin in purple bordered by a narrow white stripe on either end which is worn on the dress uniform; a smaller version of the pin which can be worn on the lapel of a civilian jacket (Senator Bob Dole used to wear this pin on his lapel); and a larger heart-shaped pin in purple with an embossed silhouette of George Washington in gold leaf.

At that time it seemed strange that because a soldier was careless or unlucky enough to get shot, that he should be rewarded with a medal, but that is the way the army does things, and I accepted the medal with pride.

Once again I was sent to an outfit that didn't need a replacement, but since I was a wounded soldier who needed to be placed somewhere, I was accepted into a communications outfit which helped foreign correspondents file their stories to the United States from cities all over Italy, such as Naples, Florence, and Rome. The stories reached the communication center by radio signals using the old Morse Code of dots and dashes and by a teletype machine, the pre-cursor of the computer and e-mail.

Since I knew nothing about sending and receiving radio signals of dots and dashes, the sergeant in charge wanted to put me in the motor pool. There I would drive various foreign correspondents to their destinations so that they could write their descriptions of the battle front. The only hitch in this plan was that I didn't know how to drive. The sergeant, who was from the south where kids as young as sixteen could drive cars and trucks, couldn't understand how a twenty-year-old man from New York City didn't drive.

"What do you mean, you don't know how to drive?" he asked.

"I live in the heart of the city," I replied. "Most people in Manhattan where I live don't drive cars. They take the subway or bus. Even if they had cars, there wouldn't be a place to park them."

At last, the sergeant in charge of the motor pool had to give up the idea of using me as a driver. Reluctantly he brought me to a British captain who was in charge of British communications, which was located in the same building as the Americans. The captain seemed impressed with the fact that I had attended college for one year. He only asked me one question: "What was your average?" I lied and told him I had a "B" average.

Satisfied, the British Captain found a job for me. I was to have night duty in the communications room, which meant that I had to listen for any teletype messages that came in overnight and let the teletype operator know that his message was being received. This didn't happen often so most of the time I slept on a folding cot all night long.

Once in a while the teletype machine would come alive with a "ding, ding, ding." The teletype machine, as if by magic, would type "Rome, RU there?"

"Yes, Ravena, GA." (Go Ahead).

Then the machine would start typing at a steady, sixty-words-a-minute pace until the entire message was completed. I would then type "Msg rcvd/LC." Eventually the message or story would be sent to the United States by mail. In the morning, I was instructed to phone a British major and tell him the number of words that were sent during the previous day. That was the extent of my duties. Following the morning phone call, I could return to my living quarters which were located in an Italian *pensione*.

In Italy a *pensione* is like tiny hotel where the proprietor and his/her family live in the building but take in a number of guests, providing them with rooms and meals for an agreed upon price. That was where the American Communications Company was quartered. It was a far cry from living in an eight-man tent, my previous living arrangements before I was fortunate enough to get shot. My room was small, just large enough to hold a folding cot and an ice box, which I filled with ice and cans of tomato juice bought at the PX in Rome.

While the rooms were miniscule and plain, the food that was served was plentiful and delicious. The cooks were able to make tasty meals even from the powdered eggs that the army supplied.

Our *pensione* boasted a gameroom consisting of a ping-pong table on which we played after lunch and supper. I became a fairly good player and developed a "slam shot" that most players could not return. However, one soldier was able to return the hardest shot I could manage. In fact, he deliberately gave me easy shots that I could slam, but he always returned them and easily won every game.

Another kind of recreation that I enjoyed in Rome was going to its magnificent opera house. The price of admission seemed cheap by American standards, so I went quite often to see and hear operas by Verdi, Puccini, Bizet, etc. The Italians were avid enthusiasts of opera and when a performer sang an aria particularly well, they would not only stand up, clap and shout "Bravo!" or "Brava!" but they would not stop their cheering until the performer repeated the entire aria.

One afternoon the opera house was taken over by the USO, a service organization that brought entertainment to the troops. On that particular day the entertainment was none other than Frank Sinatra, who was just beginning his career as a singer with Tommy Dorsey's band. Later he became a recording artist on his own. His crooning style which emphasized the lyrics of the song as well as its melody appealed to the young girls in the States who were known as

"Bobby Soxers" because of the style of short white sox that they wore at that time.

How this entertainer would appeal to an audience of predominately male soldiers was a question that was soon answered after his very first song. Sinatra was a gifted entertainer who sang familiar songs that were popular back home. His delivery was such that the audience thought that he actually believed the sentiment of the lyrics of his songs. He entertained the packed house for hours. I think the highlight of his performance came when he sang "Ole Man River" from Jerome Kern's "Show Boat."

This is a song that is usually sung by a broad-chested bass baritone like Paul Robeson. When the song was first announced, I thought that this skinny, soft-voiced crooner could never handle the range and power demanded by the song. However, I was surprised by Sinatra's ability to reach both the low and high notes of the song. I was amazed at the power of his voice when he came to the song's climax. Sinatra hit the notes at full throttle and sustained them for a crashing climax that brought the house down. The audience stood, clapped, cheered and whistled in appreciation of the truly gifted singer that was Frank Sinatra.

While the British and the Americans shared a building for communications and worked together to help journalists get their stories to their respective countries, they did not mingle socially. One day, however, the British soldiers invited some Americans, including me, to high tea.

High tea in that instance occurred at four in the afternoon. All sorts of cakes, cookies, and muffins with jam or margarine were served along with the tea. The Americans learned that this kind of tea party happened every day at exactly four p.m. Except for vital or emergency work, all activity is stopped at this hour and the soldiers have their tea and crumpets and socialize for a half-hour or so. Then everyone helps with the "wash up" and returns to work. I can't speak for the other American guests at this tea party, but it struck me as such a civilized and sensible custom that I wondered why such a routine had not yet taken hold in America.

CHAPTER NINETEEN

The war ends and I head home

WHILE I WAS ON LIMITED DUTY in the communications room, the armies of Russia, Britain, and America were rushing toward Berlin. Adolph Hitler had disappeared and, on April 30th committed suicide in his secret bunker.

Then, in May 1945, the German government unconditionally surrendered to the allied forces. I do not recall how we celebrated VE Day, but I remember thinking about how soon we could return to our civilian lives.

Since returning a huge number of soldiers to the States was a considerable

Contributed photo
Larry Cohen
in uniform, 1945

logistical problem, the army developed a point system for determining the order of redeployment back to the States: those who served the longest would be given so many points. Those who were in combat received so many points, and those who were wounded received additional points.

My total service in the army was not very long: two years and seven months. However, I did get additional points for being in combat, even though our battle lasted only fifteen minutes, and I received additional points for being wounded and receiving the Purple Heart. Therefore, I was soon on a ship carrying me back to Fort Dix, New Jersey where I received my honorable discharge papers which stated in part that: *Lawrence H. Cohen 32 896 636 private First Class, 3rd Infantry Division Army of the United States is hereby Honorably Discharged from the military service of the United*

States of America. This certificate is awarded as a testament of Honest and Faithful Service to the country (14 December 1945).

As I headed to the Bronx to live with my Aunt Lillie I had mixed feelings. I was happy to be out of the army and home among my friends, but a little uneasy because of the uncertainty that the future would hold for me. There were no parades with cheering crowds when I crossed over from the army to civilian life.

I took the subway to the Bronx wearing my olive drab uniform with a bulky winter coat complete with brass buttons. All my army belongings were carried in a green duffel bag.

Aunt Lillie greeted me with coolness. She had gotten used to living alone and was not too thrilled to learn that I intended to live with her for a while. However, her strong sense of duty and responsibility, which led her to be the caretaker for her aging mother until the latter died, trumped her desire to live alone, so she let me stay.

My next problem was financial. How could I earn some money for incidental expenses? I was too old to receive an allowance from anyone so I had to find a job. I decided to return to my old job as counterman for Whelan's Drug Store.

When I went to their employment office, I learned that they had no record of my previous employment, so I would have to apply all over again by filling out forms and starting at the bottom of the ladder. I had expected a warmer welcome from this company, but I had failed to realize that in the early forties there was a shortage of workers due to the draft and the coming war. Now the returning workers were looking for jobs so there was no longer a scarcity of workers. The companies could pick and choose and hire the most experienced workers. I decided, therefore, to look for other work.

When I was discharged at Fort Dix, I told the soldier clerk who was filling out my papers that I had worked as a teletype operator, a bit of an exaggeration since I only received messages and signed for them. However, the clerk had no way of knowing my qualifications, so he noted on my discharge papers that I was a "Teletype Operator."

I took my papers to AT&T, and tried to talk my way into a job as a teletype operator. However, unlike the soldier clerk who took my word that I was indeed a teletype operator, the manager at AT&T wanted to test my skill as a typist. He told me to take a seat in front of a typewriter that had blank keys; there were no letters marked on the keys. He asked me to type a message on the typewriter with blank keys. I had learned touch typing in the sixth grade, but I had not kept up my skills in typing, so I managed to type most of the message correctly, but that was not good enough for the personnel manager. He then offered me the least skilled job they had: the job of messenger. I would deliver messages throughout the huge building wearing roller skates.

Desperate to find work, I accepted the job, but as I was about to fill out the application forms, the man asked me, "By the way, do you intend to go to college?" Thinking that attaining a college education would be an asset, I replied, "Yes, I intend to go to college."

"Oh, I'm sorry," the man said. "We want people who will stay with the company for many years, and we learned that college graduates don't stay with our company. They tend to look for other jobs."

With those words another job opportunity was closed to me; even a lowly messenger job was out of my reach.

While unsuccessful at finding a job, even at the entry level, I decided not to worry about my finances and pal around with my friends, most of whom were former Boy Scouts like me. Many of us returned from the war relatively unharmed, except for one enterprising scout named Lenny Sternfels who had been the editor of our scout newspaper, *The Palm Leaf*. We soon learned that this young man had been killed in action. Even though he was not among our group of friends who hung out together, we liked him a great deal and mourned his loss.

The "we" in this case meant a group of boys who had been Boy Scouts, had gone to war and returned as young men. I had expected that after the war we would resume our old habits and hang out together. However, we all had reached the age when young men discover that there is another sex out there and its members are worthy of our attention. And so my friend Laurie became Mimie and Laurie; Dick became June and Dick; Kuzy became Marilyn and Kuzy, and Bob became Pennie and Bob. Not to be left out, I decided to court Celia Grossman, the young lady who had written me so frequently and faithfully when I was in the army and who had sent me homemade cookies.

It occurred to me that any young lady who would do all of that for me during the war was sending me a not-too-subtle hint that she was interested in me. Not soon after I was discharged, I called on Celia and made a date. I do not recall where we went on that first date, but I do recall going to a basketball game to watch CCNY play. I also remember attending an evening concert at Lewisohn Stadium at City College where we watched a young Leonard Bernstein lead the New York Philharmonic in a concert under the stars. Soon we were an item known as Celia and Larry. Then we began to double and triple date with our friends.

In those days, the 1940's, tickets to Broadway shows and plays were not expensive, especially if you were willing to sit in the balcony, so we saw many plays and shows together.

Soon the friendship between Celia and me reached another level when she invited me to have dinner at her house and to meet her family. While I agreed immediately, I contemplated this meeting with dread and foreboding. What would this family think of me, a person without a job, with no prospects, as a companion for their Celia?

Fortunately, the family, consisting of her mother, father, brother and sister-in-law and her grandmother, did not seem to care about my poor status or lack of accomplishments. They seemed to trust Celia's judgment and welcomed me into their family. It was a family of hard-working, well-educated Russian immigrants who were struggling to raise a family and make a better life for themselves and their children.

Sarah, Mrs. Grossman, came from a poor Russian family

whose desperately destitute mother gave Sarah away to be raised by another family. When she grew up and later married, Sarah at first stayed home, devoting herself to raising her two children, Saul and Celia. But when her children were old enough, Sarah took a job as a sewing machine operator in order to supplement the family income. Part of her sewing assignments involved making curtains, drapes and chair covers. When she learned how to sew all those home decorations, she opened up her own little shop on 66th Street and Broadway, where Lincoln Center now stands. She bought a few sewing machines and hired a couple of sewers and one installer to hang the heavy draperies that were ordered. Her son, Saul, helped with the installations and drove her around the city in the family's used station wagon because Sarah could not master the skill of driving. Her business grew, largely by word of mouth, and some of her clients were famous movie stars, like Ralph Bellamy and Marlene Dietrich. Since Sarah spent most of her time in her business, she had little time to attend the movies and so did not know that she was dealing with a famous movie star. She would only find out that her client was famous when she told her family whom she was working for. "He's a very nice man," she would say at the dinner table. His last name is Bella...something."

"You mean Ralph Bellamy?"

"Yes, that's the one. Do you know him?"

And so it went. Sarah treated all her customers alike, no matter their fame of lack of it. Apparently she did good work because her business grew. However, it never reached the point where she could hire more workers and find an assistant to share the hard work involved in interior decorating. More clients meant that Sarah had to work harder and longer hours. Often she would come home by subway at eight or nine o'clock in the evening exhausted, but the next morning she would be the first one up, ready for another day of work.

While Sarah came from a poor family, her husband Nathan was fairly well off in Russia before the Revolution. He was the owner of a fish processing factory and was comparatively well to do when he married Sarah in Russia. When the Revolution came the government took away his factory so Nathan decided to take his family to America. One of the first things he packed was his top hat and coat tails, which he intended to use while going to the opera in America, an outfit that he seldom if ever used while working in his fish store. He was indeed a cultured man who could speak three or four languages. He taught himself how to speak English by buying several English language newspapers and comparing the stories with a Yiddish newspaper which he could read fluently.

Saul, Celia's older brother, had dark brown eyes, dark hair, and a muscular build. He played the role of the family's enabler. He drove his father early in the morning to the Fulton Fish Market where his father picked out his supply of fresh fish. Then he helped his father load the fish and ice into the station wagon and drove back to the fish market near 145th Street and Broadway where he helped his father bring the ice and fish into the market.

Somehow Saul managed to help his father with the fish business and his mother with her decorating business while attending City College, where he received his bachelor's and master's degrees. Later on he enrolled in Yeshiva University and obtained his Ph.D. in psychology. While all this was going on he got married to Rosalind Holstein (Roz) who bore three children, David and Rena, twins, and then Allan.

Roz had met Saul through her sister Beaty (short for Beatrice). Roz had deep dark eyes, dark brown hair and a trim figure. She had a regal bearing which led my friend, Phil Larkin, to name her "The Duchess." Saul and Roz got married just before World War II.

Roz had a beautiful singing voice which she used to entertain the family. She sang arias from operas while Celia accompanied her on the piano. If the family had no time to go to the opera, the opera came to them after dinner as Roz sang the various operatic arias from Verdi and Puccini.

As was the case with many young mothers at that time, Roz stayed at home and took care of her three children. She, Saul and her children formed an extended family at first by living one flight above Sarah and Nathan who were happy to play the role of babysitters when Saul and Roz wanted to go out in the evenings. Father Grossman had a special talent when he acted as sitter for the twins. He could take a crying baby in his arms and like magic the baby would stop crying and go to sleep. Nathan was nicknamed "The Killer" for this special talent.

In the summer on the weekends the entire family, including me, would pile into the red station wagon with wood trim and head for Rockaway Beach where the younger generation would frolic in the ocean and look for shells on the shore. The twins, Rena and David, would refer to the shells and pebbles which they found as "beauty stones."

The long ride to and from the beach was not always smooth, for the red station wagon was like an old workhorse. Whenever we hit a bump in the road, young Rena would tell her father, "Don't go over the bumpy road."

The long rides might have been boring for the twins if not for the songs that they sang to amuse themselves. Since the young twins were just learning to talk, they had their own special titles for some of the songs we sang.

"Oats, Peas, Beans and Barley Grow" became "O.P. Beans," and "The Drunken Sailor" became "Dunkin Sailor."

I think those days of summer were happy times for the three generations of the Grossman family and for me as well.

The oldest member of the family at the table was a petite elderly lady with gray hair worn in a bun and blue eyes who was called "Bobe." Although Eva Koretz was not really Sarah's grandmother, she was treated as such, for she had helped raise Sarah in Russia, and when the family decided to emigrate to America, they took Bobe with them. Bobe had her own room in the apartment and spent most of her time there so as not to intrude. She was an educated woman who was fond of reading Russian magazines and a Yiddish newspaper, *The Daily Forward*.

Since all family members left the house in the morning for work or school it was Bobe who took care of the apartment cleaning, and cooked dinner for the family when they returned in the evening.

As it turned out, Bobe was my friend at court when I started dating Celia. She seemed to like me because she knew that, when my Grandmother was alive, I used to take her to temple every Saturday morning.

Bobe, who also attended Saturday morning services, thought that any young man who took his grandmother to the temple was a *gut neshoma*, a good soul, so she put in a good word for me when the family decided whether I would be a suitable partner for Celia.

Chapter Twenty
A natural progression

WE VETERANS WHO RETURNED FROM World War II were changed in our outlook. The war experience had converted us from fun-loving youths to serious-minded adults anxious to get on with our education, careers and marriage. Each of us, Laurie, Kuzy, Bob and I were now "going steady" with our young ladies, Mimie, Marilyn, Pennie, and Celia, each of whom had written to us so faithfully while we were in the army.

It seemed natural that our relationships would progress from being good friends to going steady to becoming engaged and finally to getting married.

I am not sure of the order in which we were married but eventually we all said our "I do's" and settled into apartments wherever we could find them, which was no easy task right after the war because so many other couples were doing the same thing.

After their honeymoon, Laurie and Mimie settled into a tiny apartment on West 23rd Street in Manhattan. Dick and June soon followed, but I can't recall where they found living quarters. Bob and Pennie also made the transition from engaged to married and managed to find an apartment in Jackson Heights in Queens.

Kuzy and Marilyn followed suit and took an apartment around 33rd Street on the west side of Manhattan. Their apartment, which may have been built in the early nineteen hundreds, had a peculiar feature: it had the bathtub located in the middle of the kitchen floor.

In the days before modern plumbing, the bathtub had no pipes connected to it to bring water into the tub. Water was heated in a kettle on the kitchen stove and poured into the tub along with cold water until the temperature of the water was just right for the bather. That is why the tub was in the kitchen near the stove which heated the water. Kuzy and Marilyn covered the tub and decorated the cover so that it served as a bench for visitors.

I never formerly proposed to Celia. We had been going together for a number of years before and after the war, and we had attended the weddings of all our friends. One day Celia asked me, "When are we going to get married?"

I don't remember how I responded to this question, but my sentiments were that, "I do want to marry, Celia, but I want to wait until I have a job."

At this point I had no idea what career I wanted to pursue. I was attending City College, under the G.I. Bill of Rights, which provided free tuition, books and supplies plus a small stipend for veterans who returned from the war. I had started out wanting to be a civil engineer, but since I flunked the first math course I took, I had scratched civil engineering off my list. Then I decided that I would like to be a journalist and took a class in journalism only to learn that jobs in that field were scarce.

Although I could write fairly well, there were other students in the class who were far better than I, so I changed course once again. My next choice was to become a Foreign Service Agent and work for the State Department. Therefore I took a course in Russian to supplement my skills in Spanish and French. However, even though the course was taught by a granddaughter of Leo Tolstoy, I did not do well in mastering the Russian language. Another option was scratched from the list of possible careers.

At this point I was drifting in a sea of uncertainty. I was just taking courses without any clear direction when my friend Laurie came to my rescue. Laurie's older sister, Sybil, was dating a handsome, well-built gym teacher named Harold Sklar. It was he who convinced Laurie to study to become an elementary school teacher. Laurie was convinced and, good friend that he was, attempted to convince me that I, too should become a teacher in the elementary grades.

The conversation that day between Laurie and me went something like this:

Laurie: It's a great job. You get lots of holidays during the year and you get the whole summer off.

Me: That's great, but I don't know anything about teaching.

Laurie: So you'll learn. That's why they have education courses.

Me: I don't know. I don't think I'm cut out to be a teacher.

Laurie: Cut it out, schmuck. Take a few courses and see if you like them. What have you got to lose?

Me: Okay. I'll give it a shot.

And so Harold Sklar convinced Laurie and Laurie convinced me to become a teacher, but there was something else besides Laurie's arguments that helped me decide. As I walked the halls of the College going aimlessly from class to class, I noticed a group of young women who were carrying charts on tag board to their class. These charts and made up games were meant for their make-believe classes in elementary school. They were learning how to teach and the charts and games were designed to interest their students.

As I passed them in the hallway, I envied them, for they knew exactly what they wanted to do with their careers. They had a sense of direction which so far had escaped me. How I wished that I could have such certainty! Now, together with Laurie's enthusiastic arguments, I had a goal to pursue. A decision had been made.

All of these thoughts went through my mind as I thought about Celia's question, "When are we going to get married?"

My plan was to finish college, pass the test for a teaching certificate, get a job as an elementary school teacher, and then get married. However, "What if I don't succeed in any one of these goals?" I worried. Celia did not seem worried at all.

"What if I don't graduate with a degree? I asked.

"You'll graduate," Celia answered.

"Suppose I don't pass the test for my teacher's certificate?"

"You'll pass the test," she assured me.

"Maybe I won't be able to find a teaching job."

"You'll find a job. Don't worry."

Then it became clear to me that Celia had enough confidence

in our future for both of us. We agreed to become engaged. Celia informed me at that time that there was another step that had to be taken before we could formally announce our engagement. I had to get permission to marry Celia from her father, the head of the Grossman household.

"There is no use arguing about it," Celia told me. "This has to be done."

Although asking for Celia's hand in marriage from her father seemed awkward, I consented.

The next night I was invited to dinner at the Grossman house. As we sat down to the table, I spoke to her father.

"Mr. Grossman," I began, "I want to marry your daughter. I love her very much and I will take good care of her."

Mr. Grossman nodded in approval, shook my hand, and offered me a drink of schnapps. The tension eased and Celia and I became formally engaged.

Contributed photo
Wedding day:
Larry and Celia

Celia's mother, Sarah, was adamant about setting an early date for our marriage. "I don't believe in long engagements," she said, as she dashed my hope of a long protracted engagement until I got a job.

Arrangements were made and the date of September 7, 1947 was set. The wedding was to take place in the temple on 149th Street between Broadway and Riverside Drive where I had been Bar Mitzva'd and where I had taken my Grandma Fannie to temple.

All the arrangements for the wedding were handled and paid for by the Grossman family, who were not wealthy but were more than willing to subsidize a traditional Jewish wedding for their daughter and me.

Aside from showing up at the wedding, my only responsibility for the wedding was to find a hotel room for our honeymoon of one week in Canada. I wrote to one hotel in Canada and received a reply that they were fully booked for the week that we wanted. Then I wrote to another hotel which replied that they "catered to only a Christian clientele."

A third hotel was less blunt in refusing our booking by noting that there were Christian churches nearby.

Finally a man who owned a ski lodge in the Laurentien Mountains in Canada, called Nyamark's Lodge, accepted us without mentioning any sort of religious requirement for using his facilities. Apparently he was a good businessman who figured that rather than have his ski lodge empty until the winter ski season began, he could accommodate couples in the interim. By this time our wedding ceremony and honeymoon plans were complete.

I remember some parts of our wedding quite vividly. For example, I remember how happy I was to see my Dad who came all the way from Florida. My Uncle Kuba, Aunt Anne's husband, would have said, "Come in; the place is crawling with aunts," for seated on the left side of the Temple were Aunt Lillie, who helped raise me when I was young, Aunt Mamie, who remembered my birthday and gave me an allowance for "spending money," and Aunt Anne, who gave me my first job as a babysitter for her only child, Enid Ruth Hammer.

This New York delegation was augmented by my aunts from West Virginia. There was Aunt Bessie, who housed me during the summer months when I worked for the Standard Furniture Company owned by Uncle Harry Pollock, the husband of Aunt Selma, who was also in the Temple.

From Pittsburgh came Aunt Dora, who not only raised my sister, Esther Ruth, but together with her husband, Uncle Ben, treated me to two summers of day camp where I met counselors who acted as father substitutes and served as role models for me.

My Dad and my aunts, by their presence at the Temple for my

wedding with Celia, demonstrated that a child can be raised by a committee of relatives and foster parents, and with a little luck, he will not turn out too badly.

Celia wore a traditional white wedding gown with puffy sleeves. I wore a light blue suit with a felt fedora hat. Before the ceremony, the rabbi called us into his office to sign the marriage contract which contained our names in English and in Yiddish. I think Celia's name came out in Yiddish as *Tzippi Dvoah* and mine was *Laib Hirsh*.

I also remember saying, "I do," and smashing the glass with my right foot. The smashing of the glass symbolizes the destruction of the temple in Jerusalem.

After the ceremony we went into another room where we blessed the bread and wine and enjoyed a buffet supper. Following the buffet there was dancing to the music of Ruby Melnick and his band. The room came alive as celebrants formed large circles, joined hands and danced the traditional *hora*. Then someone broke the circle and formed another circle around the first circle while Ruby and his band kept up a lively rhythm.

While the assembled guests were dancing, some of the men brought two wooden chairs over to Celia and me. They told us to sit and then raised the chairs over their shoulders and carried us around the room, like a king and queen on a throne. It was a rocky ride because the chairs tilted back and forth as the chair-bearers pranced around the room. Late into the night our wedding guests danced, but finally Ruby and his band packed up their instruments and the revelry ended.

Soon after the wedding we took a train to Canada. We were so naive that we didn't realize that you had to reserve in advance if you wanted to sleep in a berth on the train. When we arrived at Penn Station, we were told that there were no berths available.

We slept on the train in an upright position with only a rented pillow to rest our heads, but we didn't seem to mind. I am not sure how long the train ride lasted, but we eventually reached the station in Canada which was near Nyamark's Lodge.

A taxi soon deposited us at a series of log cabins in which three other honeymoon couples were living. Our cabin was spacious and airy with a large double bed, comfortable chairs and a set of bureau drawers. In those days there were no television sets in hotel rooms. The view from the large window was a vast green grassy field.

We met the other couples at lunch and soon became fast friends since we were all newly wedded couples on our honeymoon. There was another Jewish couple, Midge and Marty, who it turned out lived not far from where we eventually were to live in Little Neck. Then there were the Barrs, Lillie and Larry. Larry Barr worked in television as a camera man, and we often saw his name on the scroll at the conclusion of a TV show. The third couple, whose name I can't remember, were Italian and very friendly, as all of us were.

Of course Celia and I used our honeymoon for its intended purpose. We made love frequently, morning, noon and night. We had no doubt that the other couples did the same, and we greeted each other at breakfast, lunch and dinner with knowing smiles on our faces.

To describe our honeymoon week, I thought of a story I read when I took a children's literature course. In this story the main character, Homer Price, has a certain powder which when sprinkled on food makes the food taste exactly as usual, only "a little bit more so." When sprinkled in coffee, for example, the coffee tastes like coffee, only a little bit more than it usually tastes. And so it was with Celia's and my honeymoon: the food was delicious, only a bit more so.

We complimented the chef on his food, especially his soups. Finally he took us into his kitchen and showed us his secret. He kept a large pot full of meat bones which he used to make the stock for his soups. His onion soup tasted like onion soup, only a bit more so.

Our honeymoon companions were friendly, only a bit more so. The scenery of grass and rolling hills was calming and beautiful, only a bit more so.

All too soon our week of honeymoon came to an end. We exchanged addresses with our newly married friends and promised to keep in touch. I believe we had one reunion and exchanged some letters, but our lives took us on separate paths and in a few years we lost touch.

CHAPTER TWENTY-ONE

Our first home

FINDING AN APARTMENT IN New York City after World War II, when all the veterans had returned home, was no easy task. Thousands of returning soldiers were getting married and needed apartments in which to settle down and raise their families. But no one had anticipated this housing shortage problem. Since few new affordable apartment buildings had been built during the war, there was no place for most newlywed veterans and their wives to live.

Ever since our engagement, I had been looking for an apartment for Celia and me, but I couldn't find any. For weeks on end, I scanned the "Apartment for Rent" pages of *The New York Times,* but I could not find an affordable apartment. As our wedding day approached Celia and I had no place to live, other than to move in with her family. This was not a good way to begin married life. Then our luck turned.

Saul and Roz, who were living on the fifth floor of an apartment building with no elevator, were expecting a baby and needed to move, not only because of the stairs involved, but the apartment would be too tiny for their expanded family. Miraculously, Saul and Roz found a vacant apartment on the second floor of the same building where Saul's mother and father were living on West 144th Street. When they moved from East 65th Street, the abandoned apartment and all of its furniture would be ours. Celia and I now had a place of our own where we could begin our life together.

The phrase "any port in a storm" comes to mind when I think about our two-and-a-half room, five-flight walk-up apartment on East 65th Street between 3rd and 2nd Avenues in Manhattan. The apartment was in a non-descript building which had absorbed the city dust and soot for many years. The building was nestled in a row of similar looking apartment buildings. To claim some distinction from the rest of the buildings on the block, the number 326 appeared on the glass transom above the entrance.

Another distinguishing feature was the Mom-and-Pop grocery store which was run by a friendly young Jewish couple and was located to the left of the entrance. It was the kind of store where you could ask the proprietor for a can of peas and he would take a large wooden pole with a pair of grippers at the top and a spring handle at the bottom. From a high shelf where many cans were stacked he would expertly place the grippers around the can, remove it from the shelf and then release the gripper. The can of peas would drop from the pole and fall into the hand of the proprietor as smoothly and surely as the catch by a center fielder on a baseball team.

Behind the cash register was a dairy case where a large round tub of butter was located. A request for a quarter pound of butter would prompt the owner to take a large sharp knife and cut away a wedge of the cold butter which he would place on a scale on top of some wax paper. More often than not, the wedge of butter weighed exactly as much as the customer had requested.

The grocery store had another feature which Celia and I liked very much: customers could charge their daily purchases and instead of paying for every purchase they could have the amount entered into a notebook. People could pay their bill at the end of the week or when they got their paycheck.

If the tiny store was slower and less efficient than the modern super market, it was by contrast a warmer and friendlier place, where customers were greeted by name and shopping was a social event as well as a business transaction.

On the other side of the entrance to our apartment building was another establishment called the Gnome Bakery which supplied restaurants and food stores with all kinds of delicious baked goods. It emitted a mouth-watering aroma as well as a fine white dust from the flour that was used to make the baked goods. Both the aroma and the dust made their way up to our apartment on the fifth floor. The white powder joined with the black soot from our kerosene stove to make an integrated dust which no amount of dusting could completely conquer.

Our fifth floor apartment consisted of a very small bathroom, a little kitchen and a large living room, which also served as a bedroom and dining room when we had company. At night we unfolded our sofa and turned it into a bed. In the middle of the living room was a large black iron kerosene stove, which served as our main source of heat. Since we lived on the top floor, we could use a large vent pipe from the stove through the ceiling and up to the roof. In the winter our small apartment became very cold, so at night we slept under heavy down-filled comforters and blankets.

In the morning, I got up from the warm bed and lit the kerosene stove. Then I rushed back into bed and slept for another five minutes or so. It was amazing how warm the apartment became in those five minutes. The metal from the stove and the large vent pipe reflected heat in every direction. The whole apartment was bathed in warmth, except for the bathroom which was farthest away from our only source of heat. We used an electric heater for the tiny bathroom, which worked quite well.

When we were entitled to a paint job for the apartment, Celia chose a hot pink for the bathroom to make it seem warmer, but the strategy failed to convince the thermometer which registered a bone-chilling forty degrees in the morning. Our apartment had a northern exposure, and so we received little sunlight during the day. To the painter's surprise Celia chose a bright green paint for our kitchen, a color which did brighten the kitchen but displeased our landlord because it would take many coats of paint to cover over the bright green walls when a new tenant would choose a different color scheme.

In order to shave in the morning, I had to heat water in a tea kettle and mix the boiling water with cold tap water. I then shaved in the kitchen over the sink which had a mirror over the sink. Every time I shaved, I was reminded of shaving overseas in the army— where the cook would heat a large steel can of water and the soldiers would dip their steel helmets into the can to get hot water with which to wash and shave.

Another feature of our apartment house on East 66th Street was the fact that it was one of the few apartment houses in New York City that had DC current instead of alternating current (AC) which all apartment houses would eventually have. We did not fully appreciate the physics of direct current versus alternating current, but DC current had certain limitations. We could not use an electric clock, an electric refrigerator or a radio or phonograph machine because all of these ran only on AC current.

To solve this dilemma we purchased a Servel Refrigerator which ran on gas, a wind up clock, and a Philco combination radio and phonograph which could run on either direct or alternating current by flipping a switch.

Despite our lack of conveniences and our five-flight walk-up, we were quite happy in our rented apartment. We felt as Shakespeare phrased it, "Tis a poor thing but mine own." It was an inconvenient place, but it was all ours. In those days there was no shame in living the way we did. We even invited friends over for parties. When our friends were departing, we usually handed them a bag of garbage to take downstairs where the trash cans were located.

Our tiny apartment with all its faults had one advantage: it was cheap. At first we only had to pay $25 dollars a month for rent. A year later the rent was raised to $28 dollars. Even with the low rent, however, we had to struggle to meet our financial obligations. I was attending college, working toward a bachelor degree in social sciences with a minor in education. I had hopes of becoming a teacher. I was thankful that the G. I. Bill was paying for my college course work and books, as well as a minute stipend of $65 dollars a month to help with living expenses.

Celia, on the other hand, had already graduated with a degree in biology from Brooklyn College. She had found a job as a biologist with the City of New York. She worked on Ward's Island testing the sludge from various factories around the city to determine the extent of bacteria present in the waste products of these factories on any given day. Somehow with Celia's meager beginning salary and my stipend from the G.I. Bill and a disability payment for my knee and toe wounds from the Veteran's Administration, we managed to survive economically.

To help us budget our income, my friend Laurie Seidman came up with a plan that he learned while taking courses in business administration at City College. He brought us a bunch of brown bank envelopes, the kind that children used in school when the banks encouraged children to save small amounts of money every week, which the teachers collected and sent on to the bank. Laurie's budget system required us to label each envelope for our monthly expenses. There was an envelope for checking, for food, clothing, cleaning, entertaining, and miscellaneous and savings. Each month when our checks were cashed, we would deposit a specified sum of money in each envelope and hope that we would make it through the month. Generally the system worked pretty well for us and we maintained it for several years until our salaries increased enough so that we no longer needed the envelopes.

If you live and work in the borough of Manhattan in New York City, you don't really need a car. The subway and bus system can take you almost anywhere you want to go. Therefore, Celia and I had no thoughts about buying a car when Celia's father told us that there was a used car available for $90. He had seen it parked on Broadway with a "For Sale" sign on its windshield. The price seemed too good to be true, and as it turned out it was just that. We bought the car which had every illness a car could have.

The gray Buick was way past its prime and so it spent most of its remaining days in Joe's repair shop on 123rd Street between Broadway and Riverside Drive. We finally gave up on the ailing hulk and let Joe have it for some of its salvageable parts.

This experience made Celia and I think two ways about cars: One, stay away from used cars; they will usually cost more in repairs than anyone can imagine. Two, it would be nice to have a car someday when Celia and I could afford a new one.

In the meantime I had to focus on getting my bachelor's degree and passing the teacher's exam in order to get a certificate and a job. To accomplish the latter, Laurie and I enrolled in the "King Schreiber Coaching Course." We paid about $100 for the course which met weekly in a large auditorium in the city. The course consisted of going over vocabulary lists taken from previous exams, mathematics examples and problems, bits of random information that the examiners thought prospective teachers ought to know and a series of essay questions, also taken from previous exams.

King, a knowledgeable Afro-American, who eventually became a district superintendent of schools, taught the vocabulary and essay parts while Schreiber concentrated on the math. At each session we were given many pages of duplicated vocabulary questions, math examples and problems as well as essay questions which we were to answer at home and bring in the next session.

One of the most valuable parts of the coaching course was the time management chart we were trained to make before attempting to answer any questions. The chart's main purpose was to help the test taker allot a certain amount of time to each question in proportion to the number of points for that question. Taking the time to make the time management chart and sticking to its time limits would help us get the maximum number of points on the exam.

When Laurie and I finally took the teacher's exam, we were surprised at the number of questions we had seen before on the practice material. Most of us who took the coaching course and studied the hand-outs passed the exam, including Laurie and me.

We received our test scores and substitute teaching certificates in the mail. We were ready for our first teaching jobs, if we could each find one.

Chapter Twenty-Two
My first teaching job

IT DIDN'T TAKE MY FRIEND Laurie long to find a teaching job at P.S. 121 Manhattan, an elementary public school on East 103rd Street between 1st and 2nd Avenues. I'm not sure how Laurie found the job so quickly, but I suspect that his brother-in-law, Harold Sklar, who was a public school gym teacher, gave Laurie a lead. Once Laurie got the job, he told me that there was another opening in the same school.

I was interviewed by the principal, Mr. Lane, a soft-spoken fatherly figure who was anxious to balance his predominantly female staff with some male teachers. Once he saw my teaching certificate, he hired me on the spot. Normally I would have had to wait for the new term to begin before I could be assigned to teach a class, but there was a special circumstance which led to my assignment the same day. One of Mr. Lane's fourth grade teachers was leaving to get married, and she wanted to resign as soon as possible. Therefore, I was taken to the fourth grade class and introduced to the teacher who was leaving.

I thought I would sit in the back of the room and observe the interaction between the teacher and the students. However, the teacher took me aside and said, "The report cards are due before I leave, but I haven't had time to finish them. I was busy with wedding arrangements. Now, if you could take the class while I sit in the back and finish their report cards, I'll have them ready by the end of the day."

I was not prepared to take a class on the same day I was interviewed. I had no plans; I didn't know anything about the students in the class, but the teacher presented me with *Hobson's Choice*. I could either take the class so the teacher could finish her report cards, or I would have to make out the report cards myself, having no knowledge of the children or their work.

I went to the front of the room and wrote my name on the blackboard. Then I stood in front of the class with no idea what I would do. The children in their seats waited expectantly. They were unusually quiet because of the novelty of having a new teacher in the room.

After several minutes, which seemed much longer, an idea came to me. During the previous summer, I had obtained a job as a day camp counselor. In that job I had learned various games, songs, and activities that we engaged in as part of the day camp program. I decided to use some of these games and songs with the children in front of me.

I don't remember all of the activities I engaged the class in, but I do remember teaching the pupils a memory trick I had learned. The trick involved memorizing a list of ten items that would be bought in a grocery store or food market by associating a number with the food and forming a mental picture with the number and the food item. For example, I asked the class to think of something to rhyme with the number "one." A child suggested "wand."

Then I asked for an item of food that could be on a grocery list. Someone said, "eggs." "Now," I said, "make a picture in your mind combining a wand with eggs." After thinking for a while someone volunteered: "I see some eggs on the points of the wand. It looks funny." "Funny is good," I said. "Make your picture as funny as you can."

We went through ten items that way, getting a key word for each number from one to ten. For the number "two" we had "tube," for "three" we had "tree," and so on. At the end of twenty minutes the children were delighted that they could remember the ten grocery items, backwards and forward.

Then I taught them some rounds that we could sing in three parts such as "Row, Row, Row," "Three Blind Mice," "Are You Sleeping?" and an English round called, "Chairs to Mend."

I managed to keep the class busy until lunch time, and after lunch I worked with the class until their teacher had completed her report cards. At the end of the day, the teacher said "Good-bye" to her children and many of them told her that they would miss her, demonstrating how much importance children give to their relationships with adults. They don't want to close the book on their relationships even if there is a good reason for the relationships to end.

The next day, I was officially installed as a substitute teacher in the same class I had taken over the day before. Thus, the silver lining in my suddenly being thrust into teaching was that the children had gotten to know me so that we could make a smooth transition.

And so my teaching career began. For the first three years I was a probationary teacher who was expected to make mistakes, and I made plenty of them. But if a beginning teacher can manage to survive the first year, the odds are that he/she can become a good experienced teacher.

One day our principal, Mr. Lane, informed me that he would be observing me teach a lesson. He gave me two days' warning. Even though I had undergone similar "observations" during my student teaching days, I was still very apprehensive. What would I teach? What would happen if some of my students started to misbehave during the lesson? I went home that day and told Celia that I had to come up with a lesson plan for an observation during the next two days.

She thought that a lesson in Origami, the Japanese art of folding paper into various shapes, would make a good lesson and would interest the children. We could relate the folding of shapes to math with such terms as "squares," "triangles," and "diagonals."

Someone had given us a book on Origami with clear directions on how to fold paper into animals such as a bird, a duck, etc. We decided to make a bird that could flap its wings when a certain part of the paper was pulled. After I made a few Origami birds and flapped their wings, I thought that my class would be able to learn the skill as easily as I had.

On the day of the observation, Mr. Lane, the principal,

entered my room and greeted the children. Then he sat down in the back of the room. I passed out construction paper and began to demonstrate how to fold the paper into a square by making a diagonal fold and tearing off the remaining strip of the bottom edge. Although I demonstrated the procedure several times, I began to hear murmurs of frustration from my pupils. "What's a diagonal?" "My paper tore." "This is too hard." "Mine doesn't look right."

This was only the first step of the folding. How would I ever teach the more complicated folds? Mr. Lane saw the problem at once and instead of writing down all the mistakes I made in picking a project that was too difficult for my pupils, he got up and became my helper. After each fold the two of us walked around the room and helped some of the children to comply with the folding directions. Between the two of us we helped my class construct a bird with wings that flapped.

At the end of the day, Mr. Lane called me into his office and talked about the lesson. He skipped over the fact that I had not correctly gauged the abilities of my pupils. Instead he noted the possibilities of the lesson which could be integrated with math because of the various shapes that were mentioned. The lesson, frustrating as it was for many pupils, could be used for a group story on "How We Made a Bird with Flapping Wings." After the story was written on the blackboard, the children could copy it in their notebooks, which would involve spelling, penmanship and reading. Then they could take their stories home and read them to their parents and siblings, which would involve the parents in school activities.

Of course I had not thought of these possibilities when I planned the lesson originally, but Mr. Lane made me feel better about my lesson, even though it had not gone as smoothly as I had intended. Mr. Lane taught me a great deal that day about how to take group experiences such as a class trip or an Origami lesson and expand them into other learning activities like the resulting ripple of a stone dropped into a pond.

Every day at lunch time, a group of us would eat in the kindergarten room. We would squeeze into the kindergarten seats, unwrap our sandwiches which we carried in a small brown bag, and discuss whatever was on our mind. I can't recall all the names of the particular lunchroom crowd, but I remember Marty Cohen, who taught fifth grade in the room next to mine and who lived with his wife Mildred in a development called Beech Hills in Queens, not far from the house Celia and I would eventually buy in Little Neck when we left Manhattan. We used to carpool together and became good friends. Then there was Laurie, who taught on the same floor as Marty and I. Lenore Becker also taught on our floor and we soon became very good friends with her and her husband, Charley. For a week or so during the summer our two families would go camping in a beautiful campsite in Vermont.

The kindergarten teachers who hosted our daily lunch sessions were Nettie Jonath and Margaret Williams. I think Margaret was the only black woman on our staff. As far as I could tell she and Nettie were excellent teachers. Of this group, Laurie, Nettie and I were more liberal in our political outlook so we joined the Teacher's Union, which was regarded as more left-wing than the other union, the Teacher's Guild. Some of the officers of the Teacher's Union were accused of being Communists, but that was never proven. Our Union activities consisted of going to meetings in the city, picketing for wage increases and protesting unfair labor practices. But as long as the unions were divided, they had little influence on the Board of Education whose members listened politely to our demands, but voted us down every time.

It soon became apparent that a single union was needed in order to exert enough pressure on the Board of Education and the city administration. A run-off election was finally held and the teachers chose the more moderate Teacher's Guild to represent them. Eventually the Guild became the United Federation of Teachers (UFT) and it became a powerful voice for the teachers.

Those early teaching days were our formative years which brought about lasting friendships that remained strong even when we moved to distant locales and different schools. They lasted even after some of us retired from teaching; only death could break the bonds of our friendships.

When Marty Cohen retired, he and his wife Mildred moved to a home in a gated community in New Jersey called Concordia. They liked the living arrangements so much that they convinced Lenore and Charley to also move there when they retired. They tried to convince Celia and me to join them, but Celia and I had roots in our community and saw no reason to leave. However, we kept in touch by phone and visited our New Jersey friends from time to time. Marty Cohen, unfortunately, died soon after retirement; I think it was a heart attack. His wife, Mildred, died several years later from cancer. Lenore Becker developed cancer in her spine and succumbed soon after. I still am in contact with her husband Charley, who lives in Washington D.C.

Chapter Twenty-Three
Literacy testing

Laurie's brother-in-law, Harold Sklar, was right about the advantages of a teaching career. We did have nine-to-three jobs instead of nine-to-five work days; we did have many school holidays and long summer vacations. However, Harold failed to mention that our starting salaries of $1,250 a year was so low that most teachers had to supplement their salaries by taking odd jobs during the year and during summer vacations. One such job, that of a literacy test proctor, was administered by Laurie and me. In those days, the 1940's, foreign-born adults who wished to vote had to pass a literacy test, which consisted of a selection of factual information written on about a fourth grade reading level with accompanying comprehension questions. The candidates had to read the selection and answer a given number of questions correctly in order to receive a certificate which would allow them to vote. Since P.S. 121 Manhattan was chosen as a convenient testing site for the neighborhood, Laurie, Marty Cohen and I were invited to work as proctors. We gladly accepted the job in order to increase our incomes.

It was a simple task which consisted of passing out the test papers, making sure the test takers understood the instructions, timing the test, making sure that everyone was doing his or her own work, and finally collecting the papers and grading them. Those who passed the test were given "Certificates of Literacy" which allowed first-time voters to take part in the coming election. Once these new voters were enrolled, they no longer had to prove their literacy in future elections. In this whole testing process, Laurie, Marty and I were not as neutral as proctors ought to be. We were definitely biased in favor of the test takers and did our best to see that each applicant received his or her certificate, even if it meant stretching the time limit a bit to allow candidates to finish the test.

If foreign-born first voters had to pass a literacy test, it seemed only fair that the city government should provide for access to night school where English and literacy could be developed.

Offered a chance to supplement my low teacher salary, I accepted the job as a teacher at a night school in the Bronx. I believe the class met on Tuesdays and Thursdays in a junior high school in the Bronx. The students were of varied backgrounds, some young and some older. While the purpose of the class was to become familiar with spoken and written English, some of the younger foreign students came to meet friends of the opposite sex. In either case, the students were diligent and eager to learn.

The teachers would copy onto the blackboard certain fictionalized conversations which might take place at the post office, the supermarket, the bank, etc. The printed conversations came from a manual of exercises written for students who were learning to speak English. The students then copied the conversations into their notebooks and then took turns playing the roles of one of the speakers in this made-up conversation. Teachers could then point our idiomatic expressions and prepositional phrases like "standing on line," "making change," or "the price per pound."

Singing the lyrics of popular songs was another technique of immersing our students in learning to speak and write English. We would join several classes together and pass out duplicated lyrics to popular songs of the day, and the whole group of teachers and students would break out in song. It did not matter if we sang in the right key or kept time properly. We were reading the lyrics and enjoying ourselves. I remember one song we sang was "Granada." It began:

Granada, island of mystery and song...

Another technique in teaching conversational English was to hold classroom parties on special occasions like holidays and the end of the term. The students would plan the parties and bring in snacks and sodas along with phonograph records for dancing. It was a social occasion but also rich in opportunities for speaking English.

"Would you like to dance?"

"Yes, I would love to dance."

"Please pass the potato chips."

"Come dance the Rumba with me."

"I'm sorry, but I don't know how."

"Don't worry, I'll show you."

It was amazing how well our students progressed in learning to speak and write English. Most of the students came religiously to every session after a full day's work, but they were not too tired to improve their English-speaking skills. We teachers admired our students for their hard work and persistence. In turn, the students appreciated the help they received from their teachers. At the end of the term most students chipped in to buy a modest present for their teachers.

The students in the class I taught noted the worn-out school bag I carried to class each night. They decided to buy me a brand new leather school bag as a present. They presented it to me at the conclusion of our party marking the last day of the term. I thanked the class for their thoughtful gift and carried my books and papers in the shiny brown leather school bag with its brass clasp and divider pockets for many years. Today it is old and worn and gathering dust in my bedroom, but I treasure it as a fond keepsake of my days of teaching night school.

One of the best and funniest descriptions of teaching English to night school students is Leo Rosten's *The Education of H*Y*M*A*N K*A*P*L*A*N*. The asterisks between the letters represents the way this Yiddish-speaking character signed his name in all his written communications to Mr. Parkhill, his exasperated but still patient teacher. In his heavily accented English, Hyman Kaplan renders his teacher's name, Mr. Parkhill, as "Mr. Pockheel." The book is probably out of print by now, but it is a classic of its genre and represents an exaggerated and humorous way the experiences I had teaching English in night school in the Bronx.

CHAPTER TWENTY-FOUR

The long summer vacation reduced to two weeks: the day camp experience

PUBLIC SCHOOLS IN NEW YORK CITY usually end their term at the end of June. Classes don't resume until after Labor Day in September. That amounts to a two-month vacation for students and teachers. I was told that the reason for the long summer vacation goes back to the days when there were many farms all over the country. Farming families needed the children to help with the many chores involved in planting and harvesting the food that farmers grow. Therefore, the schools closed during the summer months so that the children could help with the farm work.

Even though we no longer have so many farms, and in the large cities very few farms, the custom of summer vacations for school children and staff persists, and attempts to change the school calendar have been met with resistance. However, for many teachers, especially those in the beginning of their careers, summer vacation was not an opportunity to take a cruise to Europe. It meant that the teachers had to find a temporary job for most of the two months, and so many teachers became camp counselors in the summer.

When Celia and I moved from our apartment on East 65th Street to our very own home in Little Neck, Queens, we were not far from a YMHA that was just opening up in a housing development called Deepdale Gardens. The development consisted of a large number of garden apartments built just after World War II to accommodate the returning veterans who were getting married and raising families. I heard that the Y was starting a day camp and needed counselors. When I applied for the job, I was told that since the Y was just getting started, they had no buses or campsites of their own. They had, however, made arrangements for a Y in Brooklyn to provide these facilities and to supervise our counselors. I was also told to go to the Brooklyn Y to be interviewed for a job as a day camp counselor.

Since teaching skills and skills needed to be a camp counselor were a close match, many teachers were hired as camp counselors. In addition, the schedules of teachers and counselors were also a perfect match. Sleep-away camps and day camps ran in the summer when teachers were out of school and looking for a summer job. Therefore, I was hired as soon as it was established that I was indeed a qualified teacher for the New York School System. I was told to report back to the Y in Little Neck where the counselors and I would undergo a week of training.

A social worker by the name of Abe Makofsky was in charge of our training. He was about thirty years old with a trim body and curly hair which was starting to turn gray around the edges. He always wore gray shorts and a white tee shirt with a pencil clipped to the shirt's neck band. He always carried a clip board from which we assumed came those marvelous assortment of games, songs, and stories which he shared with his young staff of counselors.

Our training days started out with a bus trip from the Little Neck Y, which at that time was operating from a rented basement in the Deepdale Gardens complex. We traveled to Van Cortland Park in the Bronx where the Y had rented several lockers which contained sports equipment like basketballs, volley balls, baseballs and bats, etc. We spent the day in Van Cortland Park playing various games with and without equipment.

In a way we did some role playing with the staff taking the part of young campers and Abe assuming the role of leader or counselor.

In those five days of training we learned many things from Abe besides games, stories and songs. We learned how to plan for a week's activities with our groups of children. We learned how to plan for a rainy day when we could not go to our outdoor campsite, which would be located in Pleasantville, New York.

We learned how to plan a bus program since we would be riding back and forth for about 40 minutes each way. We learned these skills not so much by talking about them but by actually doing them and then analyzing the process.

The highlight of our training came on a Thursday evening when we all went out to Jones Beach for a session of square dancing which was sponsored by the Parks Department every Thursday evening during the summer. That night we enjoyed the dancing and learned the various moves in square dancing like "dos-y-dos," "allemande left and right," "swing your partner," and "promenade."

In the early 1950's, I started my day-camp career which lasted for about ten summers with what was first called the "North Hills Y." The "Y" later became the Samuel Field Y and finally constructed its own building. However, for the ten years that I worked for the Y, it occupied the basement of a Deep Dale Gardens complex. During my first summer as a counselor of an all-boys group we traveled to our campsite in Pleasantville, New York which we shared with the Pleasantville Home, a kind of group home for troubled youth.

The site was a country setting with grassy fields and some wooded areas. Each group of ten or twelve boys or girls chose a name for itself and selected a campsite which would be reserved for the group throughout the season. I remember my first boys group called themselves the Pioneers. The rustic site had no laid out ball fields for volley ball courts, so we had to make our own.

Around noon we sat around our campsites and ate the lunch that the campers brought from home in their lunch boxes. After lunch we went to Long Beach for ocean bathing and playing in the sand. After bathing the children dressed in locker rooms and lined up for a custard cone at Kalin's custard stand. Then they loaded buses for their trip back home. All in all, it was a pleasant experience for the children as they made friends with one another and formed close relationships with their counselors.

Since the bus ride to and from our campsite took anywhere from forty minutes to an hour, we had a "bus program," which generally consisted of songs and games. The program in the morning usually began with a welcoming song that was probably borrowed from other camps. We sang all kinds of songs including folk songs from different countries, rounds and cumulative songs like "Bought Me a Cat" and "Bingo."

One of the games we played was called, "Telephone," a game in which the counselor would whisper a message into the ear of one camper who would in turn whisper the message to his or her neighbor. When the message had traveled all through the bus and back to the counselor who had sent the original message, the comparison of the original message with the final message was usually so different that it was cause for laughter.

Working as a counselor and then as a supervisor in a summer day camp sharpened my skills as a teacher and then as an assistant principal. I learned how to plan for interesting activities that would motivate campers and students to participate actively in the project. I learned how to motivate group morale so that campers and students would befriend and help each other. When I became a division head and then a head counselor, I knew how to listen to counselors and teachers as they discussed their problems, their successes and their failures. As for listening to counselors and teachers, I learned the art of non-directive counseling, where the listener refrains from advice giving, but reflects the thoughts of the speakers allowing them to form their own opinion about how they should solve a particular problem.

This brings me to the structure of the day camp program which promoted the concept that counselors and their supervisors should have time to contemplate on the events and learn from their experiences. The structure is designed so that each day a counselor is relieved from his or her group for a forty-five-minute rest period, but one day each week the counselor and the supervisor use one of those relief sessions to confer on a one-to-one basis. This is the time devoted to analysis of the week's events, a time to think about individual campers and the group as a unit, a time to think about projects for the future.

This conference time is where real learning takes place, where counselors' skills and insights are developed. All of this is possible because the position of relief counselor was created and freed the counselor to participate in the individual conference. While I was participating in these conferences at day camp, I did not realize how this experience would play an important part in my future.

Chapter Twenty-Five
Studying for my doctorate

WHEN I GAVE UP MY SUMMER DAY camp work, I began my studies for a doctorate in education at Teachers College of Columbia University. I took only a few courses each term because I did not want to become overwhelmed by my work as an educator and my studies at Teachers College. Eventually I reached the stage where I had to plan and execute a thesis about some aspect of education. My advisor, Dr. Margaret Lindsay, a brilliant educator, strongly suggested an empirical study rather than a historical review of the literature. An empirical study is based on an experiment which uses a hypothesis, independent and dependent variables to determine if a certain course of action produces the effect predicted in the hypothesis.

As I was searching for a suitable topic for my thesis, I thought about the way teachers are trained after they enter the education system. They have a meeting once a month from three to four in the afternoon. These meetings, however, are mostly devoted to administrative details like preparing report cards, or getting ready for teacher-parent conferences. I did know one principal who devoted time to teacher training, but his idea of training was to present a lecture for one hour while teachers remained passive and bored.

What would happen if teacher training involved the same kind of time to reflect on the week's teaching events with a non-directive supervisor as the social workers used in counselor training?

The design of my study was simple. I would administer an inventory of teacher attitudes toward pupils and teaching, the Minnesota Teacher Attitude Inventory (MTAI), to a group of teachers in our school. Then I would randomly assign half of these teachers into a treatment group and half into a control group. The treatment group would participate in six, forty-five minute sessions of non-directive counseling sessions in which they would explore the events of their teaching experiences during the week; the control group would not take part in any of these sessions. The hypothesis was that the treatment group would improve their scores on the MATAI when it would be administered again after the six conferences had taken place; the control group would show no improvement in their scores.

Scheduling and holding these individual conferences was a bit tricky. When our school was built, the architects planned for classrooms, offices, play yards, etc. However, there were no plans for conference rooms. In order to hold these conferences we had to meet in empty classrooms or book closets. Nevertheless, we managed to conduct the six individual conferences for the teachers in the treatment group.

My role during these conferences was to be non-directive and to reflect what the teacher was saying without judging or advice-giving. The results of the study were as predicted in the hypothesis: the treatment group did improve their scores on the MTAI while the control group did not. In fact, some of the control group teachers scored lower on the second administration of the MTAI than they did the first time.

I attributed this lower score to the fact that the control group was becoming frustrated by the lack of opportunity to air their ideas and feelings about their teaching experiences.

During my oral presentation of my study, I was asked if my results were not affected by the fact that a treatment group has a tendency to respond to inventories in ways that would favor the purpose of the experimenter.

This was called the "Hawthorne Effect." In an experiment in a factory in Hawthorne, New Jersey, experimenters noted that the workers responded positively to various treatments designed by the experimenter.

If, for example, the experimenter dimmed the lights, the

factory workers reported that they liked working with dimmer lights. However, when the experimenter brightened the lights, the workers said that they liked working with bright lights. The experimenter concluded that the workers liked the attention they were getting and tended to reply to the questions in a way which they thought was favorable to the experimenter. Therefore, the "Hawthorne Effect" has to be accounted for in studies which involve questionnaires or inventories.

Fortunately, I was able to theorize that if those teachers in my treatment group wanted to respond favorably to the experiment, they would answer the questions truthfully, because doing so would promote the goal of the experimenter. Eventually my study was accepted and I received my Doctor of Education degree in 1972. To mark the occasion, Celia arranged a party, and we invited all the teachers in the treatment group as well as friends and family.

Chapter Twenty-Six
Our first and only home of our own

BY THE TIME I GOT MY Ed.D. we had been living in our house in Little Neck, Queens for about twenty years. How we managed to buy our own house is an interesting story which had its beginnings in the mind of a young child who lived with his grandparents in various apartments in New York City. Apartment house living was all I experienced from age six on. However, I knew some friends who lived in houses rather than apartments, houses with green grass on front lawns and backyards. How I envied those who owned land. To my eyes they were rich people who were living the good life. My aunts in Pittsburgh and West Virginia lived in houses. I loved visiting them during the summers. I loved mowing the lawns and smelling the sweet grass when it was freshly cut. If I could grow up and have a family with a house all of our own, I would have reached an important goal in life.

So when Celia was at the beginning of her pregnancy in our five-flight walk-up apartment on East 65th Street, we started to look for a house where we could raise our family. One problem with our plan was that there were thousands of returned veterans from World War II who were also looking for houses and during the war few houses were built, so housing was scarce.

Another problem was that I was just beginning my teaching career and my beginning salary was low. In short, we were looking for a house which was scarce and we had not much money to pay for it if we succeeded in finding one.

On weekends we began our search. I don't remember how many model houses we visited, but I do remember going out to Levittown where Arthur Levitt had built hundreds of houses and was charging a modest price for them. Celia was not impressed. All of the houses were the same.

We even considered buying into a garden apartment complex that wasn't even built yet, and we made a deposit. However, we then decided that we would have to wait too long for the houses to be built, so we got our money back. One day we came across an entire block of newly built houses which interested us. There were ten houses, five on each side of the street which was named Thebes Avenue.

Some houses were ranch style houses with red brick facing, and some were ranch houses with shingle facing and expandable attics, which meant that the owners could eventually build a second story to the house if they wished to do so.

We didn't have any difficulty in choosing which house to buy since all of them were sold except one. It was a wood frame house with white shingle facing and an expandable attic, one that could be converted into upstairs bedrooms and a bathroom.

The original house consisted of a large bedroom, a big living room with a picture window facing north, a rather tiny kitchen but roomy enough to hold a round table and four chairs for dining, and a small bedroom where our two children would sleep on stackable bunk beds.

Celia and I liked the house right away. Compared to our one-and-a-half room apartment on the fifth floor of a building with no elevator, this house was our Garden of Eden. We liked everything about the house, even the little touches like a bookcase built into the door in our living room which closed off the stairs to our attic. The price for the house was $12,999, a reasonable price in those days, but still beyond our means.

However, as a veteran I was entitled to a government 30-year mortgage under the G.I. Bill, so the Dime Savings Bank of New York granted us a loan. We had to put down $500 in escrow, a sum of money we didn't have, but a distant relative of Celia's mother, whom we called Uncle Benny, lent us the money, which we eventually paid back. Our monthly mortgage payment with four and a half percent interest came to about $130 a month, an affordable sum, even though I was on a beginning salary. The loan officer at the bank granted us the loan because I had a teaching job which at that time was relatively secure. He would not grant the loan to Celia because she was expected to stay home and raise her family.

Since Celia and I had been apartment dwellers for most of our lives, we found the closing process a complicated, strange business. We met in the offices of our builder's lawyers and had our attorney with us who had worked for the Grossman family for many years. I remember signing many documents which I didn't even bother to read. Finally the legal proceeding transferring the builder's property to Celia and me was completed. At that point I was supposed to hand a bank check to the builder as a down payment on the house. However, unschooled in financial matters, I didn't know the difference between a bank check and an ordinary personal check. I only had an ordinary check, not a check written by the bank. The builder, however, graciously accepted our personal check and we closed the deal. As of that moment we were the owners of the house in Little Neck, New York, block 8217, and lot #152. We also owned a 30-year mortgage payable to the Dime Savings Bank. Eventually the Dime Savings Bank sold our mortgage to a bank in Brooklyn, The Brooklyn Savings Bank.

Chapter Twenty-Seven
The neighbors

OUR NEIGHBORS WERE ALL WHITE but from different backgrounds. They or their ancestors came from Greece, Germany, Norway, Poland, Ireland, Italy, Russia and Slovenia.

Our neighbors to our west were an older couple with no children; they were reserved but friendly. When our first son, Philip, was born, they presented him with a toy poodle dog which, when wound up, became a music box that played "Jesus Loves Me." I don't think they were aware of the fact that the musical dog played a Christian hymn. At any rate little Philip loved the toy and played the song when he went to bed. We are not certain whether the song played countless times had any effect on Philip's later religious sentiments.

Of all our neighbors, the Larkins, who lived directly across the street from us, became our closest and dearest friends. Phil Larkin, a tall broad-shouldered man with a face crowned by blond hair, was as typically Irish as one can get. He was a friendly sort who would strike up a conversation with anyone he met. One day he sauntered over to our front lawn where Celia and I were standing and started to talk. We exchanged information about our families, jobs and such and before we knew it we had become good friends. We met his wife, Margaret, who had a trim frame with brown curly hair and blue eyes. Before giving birth to fraternal twins, Joseph and Kevin, she had worked for the phone company, AT&T. Many years later, when her family was grown, she became a financial officer in the movie theater division of Viacom. She and Celia became best friends, and our children, Philip and Steve, became good friends with their children, Kevin, Joseph, Bob, Michael and Margarette.

One day Phil Larkin approached me with an idea about

building a cement patio in our backyards. He had it all planned out. We would chip in to buy a cement mixer at Sears. Then we would help each other build our patios. Even though I knew nothing about cement work or patio building, I was young and naive enough to think I could pull it off, so I agreed. As it turned out, it was not one of my wisest decisions, for it took more work than I had imagined and it took more skill than I could master. Even turning the cylinder of the cement mixer was harder than I had anticipated.

Another neighbor, Bill Ritter, who lived two houses up the block from the Larkins, was able to hook up our cement mixer to a motor which simplified the mixing of the cement. But getting the right mixture of sand to cement turned out to be a problem. Sometimes the mixture had too much cement and sometimes it had too little. Then there was the problem of what to do with the wet cement once it was mixed. No matter how I tried, I couldn't get the cement to be as smooth and even as professional cement workers could.

Fortunately another neighbor who lived around the corner came over to help. Since he was a building contractor, he knew a lot about cement work and was able to produce a smooth finish to our cement patios. Together, Larkin and I with much help from our friends were able to build our patios, which are still standing today, monuments not to our skill as cement workers, but to the community of workers who came to our aid.

Although I vowed never to touch cement work again, we enjoyed our patio for many years. Our friends, whom we called Uncle Benny and Aunt Fanny, bought us a large redwood table and benches for our patio so that we could eat outdoors in the summer. On weekends when our sons and grandchildren visited, we enjoyed our meals together, especially when the barbecue grill was fired up and grilling hot dogs and hamburgers.

Our plot of land was 50 feet wide and 100 feet long. That left us a large backyard which we could use to grow vegetables and fruits. Celia and I used the back third of our yard as a vegetable garden. We planted tomatoes, cucumbers, carrots, lettuce, corn, radishes and watermelons. Raised in the city with its concrete sidewalks, Celia and I were delighted when we planted tiny seeds from the Burpee Company and saw them grow into delicious food. Even though we were not successful with all of our crops—the lettuce didn't grow into heads, and we learned that corn had to be planted in several rows so that it could cross-pollinate—we enjoyed planting and harvesting our crops. However, as the years passed, our backyard vegetable garden grew smaller and smaller until we had only tomato plants and some raspberry bushes. In the summer months, our grandchildren loved to take little baskets to the backyard to pick the red raspberries which were tart but delicious all the same.

CHAPTER TWENTY-EIGHT
Parenting

PHILIP EDWARD COHEN

OUR FIRST SON, PHIL, was born on March 12, 1952 in the Horace Harding Hospital, a hospital that is no longer in existence. The name Philip was derived from Celia's grandfather on her father's side named Froyim. The name Edward is for Celia's acting grandmother, named Eva Koretz.

I can recall that Celia was very calm about the birth procedure as though she had gone through it several times before. I also remember that when we arrived at the hospital, its one elevator was out of order, so we had to walk up three flights of stairs. The exertion of climbing the stairs might have interrupted the birthing process because Celia's labor stopped, and I was told to go home and wait until someone at the hospital called me.

Eventually Phil made his long-awaited appearance into this world, a healthy eight pounds and change. I assumed the role of a proud father by passing out cigars to all my friends, a custom which was prevalent in those days before the anti-smoking campaign took hold. I believe Celia remained in the hospital three days before we brought our infant home and installed him in his crib in our tiny bedroom. Celia's mother, Sarah, came to live with us to help take care of Celia and the baby. She did relieve Celia of some of the late night feedings and diaper changing when little Phil woke in the night. Like Celia, Sarah knew exactly what to do whenever Phil voiced his displeasure about the way he was feeling.

Phil introduced his new family to a medical condition known as colic, a painful contraction in the abdominal area which caused him to cry loud and long. The only remedy for this was to hold and rock him gently until the pain subsided and he drifted off to sleep. Hearing young Phil start to cry in the middle of the night, Sarah would come to the rescue and comfort him until he went back to sleep. She was an enormous help in those first weeks. In time Phil's colic condition abated and he began to sleep through the night.

One of Phil's first exposures to formal education was his enrollment in a private nursery school called *Les Clochettes* ("little bells" in French). The school was run by a gentle and talented young man named George Cullinen and his wife.

As far as Celia and I could determine our son thrived in the school and seemed to have had a good time in doing so. Phil received his first diploma on June 15, 1956 for successfully completing the early childhood program.

We also enrolled him in an art course at the Museum of Art and a series of science films at the Museum of Natural History. We signed up for the "Children's Record Club," which delivered a new record each month. They were adaptations of musical compositions like "Sleeping Beauty" and "Cinderella." When Phil was old enough, we contracted for piano lessons with Edward Edson, a talented piano teacher who had been a student of Isabelle Bayman, who had been Celia's piano teacher. Phil did well with his piano lessons, practicing at home on our upright Steinway and going regularly to his Saturday sessions at Mr. Edson's studio which was part of the teacher's home.

When I think of those early years with Phil, I can picture him sitting on the floor of our living room with his electric phonograph plugged into the wall socket near the stairway to the expandable attic, which we did not expand until later. He would play his records for hours, completely absorbed. Perhaps this was the germ that grew into his love for music.

Philip at the age of five was now ready for a new experience: summer day camp. I had been working at the North Hills "Y," now known as the Samuel Field "Y" for several years and I knew it would be a good experience for young Phil. However, Phil was several months younger than the minimum age set for the youngest group, so the director asked to interview Phil to determine if he was ready for the program. When asked what made him think he was ready for day camp, young Phil replied, "I'm frong and I'm fart," a classic Spoonerism for "I'm strong and I'm smart." The director smiled and accepted Phil into the program without any further questions.

We sent Phil to the Samuel Field "Y" for many summer seasons. He enjoyed the activities and made many friends. As a teenager, he and his friends would sit in the back of the bus and sing parodies of the folk songs we sang as part of our "bus program." The trip to and from our campsite, The Henry Kaufman Campgrounds in Huntington, Long Island, was three quarters of an hour each way. As was done on many similar bus trips before, we used this time to sing songs, play games and tell stories. For example, one of the songs we taught on the bus was Woodie Guthrie's "This Land is Your Land."

Phil and his gang would parody the songs. We didn't realize then that Phil's love of parody, while loaded with humor and good fun, was also a foreshadowing of an adolescence filled with rebellion. While psychologists wrote about the adolescent stage as one of a breaking away from standard values and beliefs, Phil proved their theories in spades.

Of course the Vietnam War added fuel to the flame of rebellion on the part of teenagers. Our government was telling its teens that as soon as they graduated high school, they were invited (drafted) to go to war in some foreign land called Vietnam. The teenagers responded with "Hell, no, we won't go."

In a way Phil's colic symptoms when he was an infant returned in a different form during those years, but we couldn't relieve his pain by picking him up in our arms and rocking him gently. Like a thunderstorm with flashes of lightning and ear-splitting explosions, the chaos slowly spends itself and fades away. And so it was with Phil. One day he decided to neaten his long, flowing, black head of hair with a pony tail. It was a sign that the storm had passed.

Eventually Phil enrolled at Stony Brook University where he decided to major in music, partly because he enjoyed playing music and partly because the music department was small and intimate.

Celia and I attended his graduation ceremony, which was a low-keyed affair. I remember being ushered into a room where refreshments were being served and an instructor from the music department was playing Scott Joplin on the piano.

After graduation Phil decided to take some time off by hitchhiking alone across the country and into Canada. Celia and I argued against his plan and were fearful about his safety. However, we were unable to dissuade him even though we pointed out that a long-haired young man traveling across the country alone with a backpack and a guitar may not always receive a warm welcome in some of the conservative parts of our country.

I guess Phil wanted to prove to himself that this was something he could do—survive on his own while hitchhiking across the country. It certainly gave him plenty of time to think about what he wanted to do in life. Celia and I didn't hear from Phil very much during his walking tour. He may have called once or twice, but we still had an uneasy feeling about his safety. However, one day while we were on vacation, we received word from Celia's mother, Sarah, that Philip had returned and was eating supper at her apartment in Flushing. We were much relieved to hear about our son's safe return. Celia and I did not learn much about Philip's long trek, but he did tell us that he had some minor trouble with the authorities in one town or another because police officers didn't take kindly to strangers roaming through their streets.

As with many young men who graduate from college but do not have a career path in mind, Phil was unsure about his future plans. He tried his hand at certain manual jobs such as installing home alarm systems but he didn't see much future in them. At one time he had the idea to learn how to drive large trucks or tractors, but that idea didn't pan out, either.

We don't often think about how many of our important decisions are influenced by a powerful social force called "networking." For example, my best friend, Laurie, was guided into becoming a teacher by his brother-in-law, Harold Sklar. Then

Laurie talked me into becoming a teacher. Although I was not able to convince Phil to join Celia (who had become a kindergarten teacher) and me in the teaching profession, our friend, Phil Larkin, played a part in helping our son reach a career decision.

It happened like this. One day as young Phil was sitting on the front porch step outside our house, Phil Larkin walked over, sat down next to him and began talking. He asked our son what he wanted to do now that he had graduated and had taken his "grand tour" into Canada and back. When our son replied that he had no idea about what he wanted to do with his life, Larkin made a suggestion. He said, "I hear that they're giving an exam for postal workers pretty soon. You could pass that exam without any trouble. Then you'll have some money coming in while you're deciding what you really want to do."

It must have seemed like a good plan to someone who was searching for some kind of direction in his life, for Phil took the advice, passed the exam easily and became a United States postal worker. His plan probably was to keep the job until something better came along. In the meantime, time passed and Phil was promoted to supervisor in charge of mail delivery. There was a time when Phil was happy as a supervisor in charge of getting the mail delivered expeditiously. He had to solve the many problems which the job entailed: how to get the mail sorted, how to best use the men and women on his staff to get the job done, and how to maintain worker morale so that the team worked well together. He also had to solve the problem of how to integrate a new computer system into the mail delivery process.

MY MOTHER

I VISITED MY MOTHER AT the state hospital twice when I was a grown man.

That first visit was arranged by Aunt Ray. Aunt Ray was a loving caregiver for my mother during her entire life at the hospital. Not only did Aunt Ray visit my mother frequently, but she tried her best to keep in constant touch with me and my one surviving sister, Esther Ruth, by writing letters to both of us. Apparently she had our names and birthdays listed on her wall calendar for when my sister and I were settled in our various homes, she never failed to send us a birthday present, usually an article of clothing from a department store called Halley Brothers, where she worked as a saleswoman.

For my first visit to my mother, I brought my wife, Celia, and my son, Philip, who was two or three years old and in a stroller. We met outside the hospital on the sidewalk. I can recall how a thin woman with gray hair, neatly combed, and with bright green eyes approached us from the steps of the hospital.

At first, she wore a sad expression. But as she drew nearer, her face lit up with a smile as though an important loved treasure had been returned to her. She seemed to be emotionally overwhelmed at seeing her grown son after almost fifty years and meeting her grandson. I think there were tears in her eyes along with her broad smile.

The only other time I saw my mother was in the early 1950's when I received a letter from Aunt Ray telling me that my mother was dying. Would I come to see her one more time?

I obtained a three-day leave of absence from my teaching job and visited my mother for the last time. She was deathly ill, but she smiled when she recognized me. At least I got to say goodbye before she died.

Years later, as I thought about my fractured relationship with my mother, I realized that I should have done more to establish ties with her, to visit her, to write to her, and to send photos of our family to her. What kind of son abandons his mother and cuts her out of his life when she needs him most?

The fault was mine if blame is to be assigned. However, there were mitigating circumstances which may account for my lack of emotional warmth for my mother. As a child, I grew up without a nuclear loving family. My various caregivers were kind to me, even liked me, but they were no substitute for a loving mother, father, and siblings. As a result, I had no template for establishing a loving relationship with others; I had to learn this, step by step, in a self-taught course like "Loving Relationships 101."

One of my first lessons took place when I saw my mother's smile outside the state hospital in Cleveland, Ohio, when I visited her that first time after all those years.

STEVEN BARNETT COHEN

ABOUT TWO AND A HALF years after Phil's birth, Steven Barnett Cohen made his way into this world. His middle name comes from my grandfather, Barney Cohen, who helped raise me together with my grandmother, Fannie, and her daughter, Aunt Lillie. I have not studied the role of birth order and its effect on personality, but I do know that Steve was an easy child to raise. Celia and I were more relaxed with Steve, having spent our anxieties on our first child. For example, we didn't send Steve to art classes or enroll him in museum programs or even send him to nursery school. We just let him develop in his own way. As a result, Steven developed an easy-going personality, happy, humorous, and self-assured. Like his older brother, Phil, Steve loved to listen to phonograph records, especially a treatment of "Sleeping Beauty" and "Cinderella" by Tchaikovsky and Prokofiev, which was produced by the Children's Record Guild. In fact he played those records so many times that the needle wore out the grooves in the records and we had to order new ones.

Not only was Steve musically inclined, but he had an explorer's instinct, which sometimes got him into trouble. As soon as Steve was able to walk, we were able to take him shopping with us at Waldbaum's Supermarket which was located about a half-mile south of our house on Horace Harding Boulevard. Celia would tear off a piece of her shopping list and hand it to me so that we could speed up our shopping chore. When all our items were placed in our shopping basket, we would go to our favorite checker, Gertie, a nurturing lady who greeted our four-year-old with a lollipop each time we shopped. One day our young explorer decided to visit Gertie on his own without his parents with visions of lollipops stuck in his tiny head. He didn't bother to say, "Goodbye, Mom and Dad. I'm going to see Gertie for a lollipop. I'll be back in a half-hour or so." No, he just took off, headed due south with his eye on the prize, a lollipop from his friend, Gertie.

Upon reaching the northwest corner of Horace Harding Boulevard where auto traffic is quite heavy, Steven must have paused to consider his strategy in order to negotiate crossing the busy thoroughfare. Fortunately, the lady in the corner house on Marathon Parkway was looking out her window and saw a tottering four-year-old about to cross one of the busiest east-west corridors in all of Queens. She sprang into action, rescued little Steve, and called the 111th police precinct.

In the meantime, Steve's distraught parents searched for their missing explorer. After an hour of fruitless searching and calling his name, Celia and I called the police station to report our missing child. "Yes, he's here," said the police officer. "Bring a clean diaper."

One would think that this misadventure would have cured Steven of his wanderlust, but that didn't happen. When he was around nine, we sent him to day camp during the summer. On a trip to the Yankee Stadium to watch a ball game, Steve managed to get separated from his group. Quite calmly he called us on the telephone. "I can't find my group," he said.

"Do you see a policeman anywhere?" I asked.

"Yes, I see one."

"Well, tell him you can't find your group and he'll help you."

Once again the police department rescued our explorer.

Like his brother Phil, Steve was encouraged to take piano lessons with the same teacher, Edward Edson. Steve was a fairly good student, except for the fact that he tended to memorize the music rather than read the notes. However, his teacher was very patient and eventually prevailed upon his pupil to learn to read music as well as to memorize it. Steve took lessons for several years, but when his older brother announced that he would no longer take music lessons, Steve decided that he, too, would quit. However, Celia and I convinced him to stay with his lessons until he played at the yearly piano recital that Edson arranged at the end of the school year in June. Steven agreed to this arrangement, believing that after the recital he could retire from piano lessons. When Steve's turn came to play his piano piece, however, he played so well that he breezed through the piece with a flawless rendition, so he decided to continue his lessons for a few more years.

Meanwhile, during the summer, Steve attended the Usdan Center for Arts day camp at the Henry Kaufman Campgrounds in Huntington, Long Island. There he played tympani and jazz piano. His jazz piano teacher was Valerie Capers, a gifted instructor. Steve enjoyed the experience so much that he asked to take private lessons with Valerie in her Bronx apartment house. Once a week, Steve traveled to the Bronx where he received lessons in jazz piano. But Valerie also assigned some kind of piano music homework which involved practicing during the week before his scheduled piano lesson.

At this time Celia's mother would visit us from her apartment in Flushing. She would ask Steve to practice his piano piece for her. At the end of the exercise she would say, "Oh, that was wonderful. Play it again." Then Steve would repeat his piece and Grandma would ask for an encore. When Steve went for his weekly lesson with Valerie and played his piece for her, Valerie would remark, "Oh, I believe your grandmother was visiting this past week."

After graduation from Benjamin Cardozo High School, Steve enrolled in the Manhattan School of Music where he majored in music composition. Some of his teachers were: John Corigliano, Ludmila Ulehla, Nicolas Flagello, and Clampaolo Brazali, names that will be familiar to many classical musicians.

In order to support himself through college, Steve obtained a job as a keyboard player with a small orchestra that played for special occasions like weddings, Bar Mitzvahs, anniversaries, etc.

In those days, Steve's keyboard was a heavy and clumsy synthesizer which he had to haul to every job together with an amplifier which was also big and heavy. To move all this equipment, he used a hand truck. His uniform for these "gigs" was black pants and a jacket, and a white shirt with a black bow tie. To those who saw him loading or unloading his car, he must have looked like a truck driver in a tuxedo.

Steve enjoyed playing with his band, but he disliked hauling his heavy instruments and amps, so he looked forward to the day when he could make a living from his composition skills alone.

In about four years, Steve was able to give up his career as a band member and devote himself to composition, arranging and writing music for people who recorded their songs on tape but needed someone to score their work with musical notation.

In the days before computers that can score musical notation with a key stroke, musical notation had to be done by hand. To do this, Steve used a speedball pen and India ink. When the composition was done, Steve had a neat musical manuscript and a messy speedball pen which he washed in our bathroom sink. He was unaware at the time that the India ink which he washed from his pen had a corrosive effect on the bathroom sink so that no amount of scrubbing could erase the pattern of black crow's feet near the sink drain.

When a plumber noted the black lines ingrained in the sink, he suggested that we replace it with a new sink. However, we decided to keep the sink as-is—as a treasured relic of Steve's music composition process.

STEVE LEAVES THE NEST

IF ONE IS A COMPOSER of music and lives in New York, then Manhattan, not Queens, is the place to set up shop. Eventually, Steve rented an apartment on the West Side of Manhattan. Later on, he rented a small office near Broadway where he could work on his music and receive clients who needed some kind of musical notation, copying, or transcription services. Sometimes, a well-known music arranger became so busy that he had to subcontract some of his work to other arrangers, and Steve often found clients for musical arrangements that way.

While his career was moving along nicely, Steve decided to do something about his social life. He subscribed to one of the many dating services and noted in his autobiography that he was a music lover. That is how he met another music lover, Andrea Harris, a bright young lawyer who was a graduate from Yale School of Law. She was a petite young lady with short black hair and a lively personality. They dated for a while, moved in together, and decided to get married in Pittsburgh, Andrea's home town, on February 2, 1985.

About three and a half years later, their first son, Charlie, was born. In appearance Charlie had the build of his father and some facial characters from his mother. As Charlie grew older, he became interested in acting in the theater. He was in many school plays in high school. Celia and I, along with his parents, attended some of the plays and were impressed by his voice projection and understanding of the characters he portrayed. He also possessed a clear singing voice—all asserts for those who wish to make a career in the theater.

Almost four years after Charlie's birth, Eliot was born, a smaller version of his brother. As he grew older, Eliot was fascinated by the small hand-held computer games which were popular at that time. On frequent visits to his grandparents' house, Eliot would appear with his computer game, which seemed like an appendage to his hands and fingers. Celia and I feared that his game playing would become an addiction or that he would not have any social skills. Like his brother, Eliot liked to act in school plays and has a talent in this area. At present he is searching for a college where he can hone his acting abilities.

CHAPTER TWENTY-NINE

Grandparenting

PHILIP MET SHARON WHILE HE was attending Stony Brook University. We liked her immediately. She had long blonde hair and blue eyes, which betrayed her Irish ancestry. After graduation, Phil and Sharon moved in together into a little rented house. Eventually they decided to marry, but they did not want a traditional marriage ceremony. Instead they opted for a ceremony in a secluded part of a public park called the "Duck Pond."

On November 17, 1981, our first grandchild was born to Phil and Sharon. Not wishing to offend either the Irish or Jewish side of the family, their parents named their first child Nova, after the term for a star that becomes brighter in the sky.

At that time Sharon was working at a bank. After her maternity leave was over, she needed to provide day care for Nova while she returned to her job at the bank.

To accomplish this, she prevailed upon various cousins to take care of Nova for one or two days a week. Since I had retired in 1978, I volunteered to take care of her every Thursday. Early each Thursday morning, Sharon would deliver Nova to our house along with several bottles of breast milk and a baby carriage. Then Sharon would take off for work. Celia at that time was still working as a kindergarten teacher, so Nova and I kept each other company until Sharon returned around four o'clock to pick up her daughter.

Nova proved to be an easy baby to care for. She seldom cried and took several long naps in the morning and afternoon. When she was awake, I took her for a carriage ride up and down the streets of our block. Sometimes we visited an elderly couple who lived in the corner house up the block. They regarded Nova as they would their own grandchild. They always had a batch of homemade cookies which, as Nova grew older, they offered whenever we dropped in for a visit.

At lunchtime Nova and I enjoyed a bowl of soup. I thoroughly enjoyed our Thursdays together and even though Nova may have been too young to remember those experiences, we, grandfather and granddaughter, had a chance to bond in a loving relationship. I think this arrangement went on for about a year when Sharon decided that the daily farming out of her first-born was too burdensome for the meager amount of money paid by the bank. She decided to become a "stay-at-home Mom," and so ended our Thursday playdates.

Celia and I watched Nova grow from a toddler to a young girl as she often came from Long Beach, New York, where she lived with her parents, to visit us in our Little Neck home. As a youngster, Nova was fond of playing with some large toys kept in our backyard shed. It was built of wood by Celia's brother, Saul, who also made the wooden rocking horse which all of our grandchildren used when they were young. Besides the homemade rocking horse was a wooden spring board that was great for bouncing up and down. Nova liked to bounce on the spring board and dismount onto the backyard lawn shouting, "Ta-Da!" whereupon we would all applaud.

When Nova grew old enough to attend day camp, she also attended the Usdan Center for the Arts, where we had sent her Uncle Steve. We knew it would be a good experience for her. She majored in violin and played in the orchestra, where we were guests at the final recital. Both her parents and grandparents were so proud to hear Nova play such beautiful music with the orchestra. She attended Usdan for several seasons and then decided to get a summer job to earn some money on her own.

After graduating from high school, Nova went to Smith College in North Hampton, Massachusetts where she majored in government. Upon graduation she obtained an intern position with Congresswoman Carolyn McCarthy. A photograph of Nova standing next to the Honorable Carolyn McCarthy stands atop our cabinet in the little room adjacent to our den. Nova is now a young woman who works for the Democratic National Committee as a consultant and researcher for Democratic candidates who are running for office. She resides in an apartment in Washington, D.C. and enjoys her career.

After Nova came Derrick on June 22, 1984. It might be said that the phrase "he followed his own drummer" was coined to describe Derrick as a young boy and teenager. He was good at what he liked to do, but followed his own beat when it came to meeting deadlines and getting with the program. He had a talent for drama, appearing in several plays at Usdan Center for the Arts. He was good at math and a whiz with computers. His chosen college was The Ringling Brothers School of Arts and Design, which proved to be a good fit for his talents and temperament. His portfolio at his graduation from the college revealed his artistic capabilities and his keen eye for design.

About six years after Derrick was born, Coral made her appearance on July 10, 1990. She turned out to be petite with brown hair and brown eyes. She has the body and the grace of a dancer, but she has also mastered the art of playing the recorder, flute and oboe.

As she grew older, Coral began to take dancing lessons, sometimes enrolling in two different classes during the week. Coral often can be seen practicing a dance routine all alone without music, just doing the steps to a rhythm she carries in her head. Like her sister, Nova, and her brother, Derrick, Coral attended the Usdan Center for the Arts where she majored in dancing, as one might have guessed.

HERMAN COHEN (1896-1984)

FOUR MONTHS AFTER DERRICK'S birth, I had to mourn the death of my father, Herman Cohen, who would have been eighty-eight years old had he lived until his next birthday in April 1984.

Near the end of his life, my Dad had been living in a nursing home in Whitestone, Queens. He was suffering from lung cancer, probably as the result of a long-time smoking habit. Although he had kicked the habit ten years before his death, his lungs were too damaged for his illness to be reversed.

In the middle of the night on October 3, 1984, I received a call from the nursing home that my father had died his sleep.

As a child, I was disappointed with my father for deserting my mother when she was placed in a state hospital and for placing me in the care of grandparents, aunts, and other caregivers. As I grew into adulthood, I learned not to judge him, but to accept him the way he was. He had played the hands he was dealt without complaining. As a soldier, he went through the First World War; then he suffered through the Great Depression of 1929 and the breakup of his family. He mourned the death of his father and, soon after, the death of his mother. He tried to manage the properties that his father had left him but the buildings were tenements in need of repair so he had to sell them off.

He saw his son go off to World War II and dealt with it by writing letters and sending salamis from the corner delicatessen. During that war he trained and studied to become an airplane mechanic but with the war's end, his job opportunity ended as well.

After the war, we lived together for a while in his one room at the Hotel Empire on West 65th Street near Lincoln Center. Sometimes we heated up soup over a hot plate, and sometimes we went out to a restaurant. One of our favorite dishes at a local restaurant was "chicken in a pot," a portion of chicken in broth of chicken soup which was cheap but nourishing.

Perhaps my Dad dreamed of living in a place where there were no cold winter winds, but his ability to do so was remote until fate dealt him a winning hand. Dad was riding in an automobile with a friend one day when a large truck hit their car and totaled it. Fortunately no one was severely injured and the company that owned the truck made a substantial settlement out of court.

My father used the money he received to rent another room in a modestly priced hotel in Miami Beach, Florida on Collins Avenue. He enjoyed mild weather during the winter months and an air conditioned room during the hot summer months. From time to time, we exchanged letters and one summer, Celia and I drove to Miami Beach to visit him.

ILLNESS

IT SEEMED THAT DAD was content with his retirement in Florida until one day I received a call from my cousin, Janet Davis, Aunt Dora's daughter from Pittsburgh who had also retired to Miami Beach. She told me that my father was in the local hospital having fainted on the way to the supermarket.

By the time I was able to fly to Miami Beach, my father was out of the hospital but confined to his bed in the hotel room. He seemed to be very weak and unable to walk. My intention was to stay overnight in my father's hotel room and then bring him home to New York. However, my Dad refused to leave his hotel room in his weak condition. We then had to go to Plan B. I would stay with him until he felt strong enough to make the trip.

Celia was not thrilled with the prospect of my staying in Miami Beach for a week or more but she understood that there was no alternative.

And so, as is the case with so many elderly sick parents, the parent-child relationship is reversed whereby the child takes care of the parent.

Each day I prepared his meals, heating food over an electric burner. Then I held him by the arm and walked him down the long hotel hallway outside his room in order to exercise his joints and make him stronger for the airplane journey to New York.

In about five days, Dad felt strong enough to make the trip. We arranged for a wheelchair with the airline so that Dad would not have to walk to and from the airline gate.

After Dad was living in our house a few days, we took him to a doctor for a complete examination and learned that he had an advanced case of lung cancer. Nothing could be done for him except palliative care.

We found a nursing home in Whitestone, Queens that was able to care for my Dad. Celia and I visited him as often as we could. One time we took our granddaughter, Nova, to see him. Dad seemed happy to see his great-granddaughter. Toward the end, my father and I became closer than ever. I had reached the point in our relationship where I became less judgmental and did not require my father to live up to my expectations of what a father should be. We could finally accept each other just the way we were. My father died peacefully in his sleep on October 3, 1984.

CHAPTER THIRTY
Celia

Contributed photo
Larry and his wife Celia

MY UNCLE KUBA, AUNT ANNE'S HUSBAND, was a professor of Latin and Greek at Hunter College. When Aunt Anne invited the family over for some kind of celebration, Uncle Kuba would answer the door and say, "Come on in, the place is crawling with aunts." Aside from that little joke, this Latin and Greek scholar had little to say to the assembled aunts and uncles, and they in turn had little to say to him.

However, when Celia came into the family, Uncle Kuba found someone with whom he could talk about Cato, Cicero, Sophocles, Plato, Socrates and Euripedes. Not only was Celia a voracious reader, but she retained almost everything she read. She would visit our local public library, take out five or six books and finish them before they were due. Then she would return the books and start the process all over again. At night, when Phil and Steve were in bed, she would stretch out on the couch in our TV room with a book in her hand and read while watching TV, multi-tasking even before the word was coined.

If she was not reading then she was doing some kind of embroidery in which she would follow a rather complicated pattern designed by Erica Wilson and create beautiful designs and pictures from lengths of wool yarn which she purchased from Smiley's Yarn Shop in Jamaica, New York. Celia and our across-the-street neighbor, Edna, would make frequent trips to the shop and bring home large bags of wool yarn that eventually became beautiful tapestry which, when framed, would grace our walls or be made into pillows for our sofas. The framing was done in Peggy's Custom Framing Shop in Bayside where Celia was a frequent customer. The shop is still doing business today although the original owner, Peggy, and her husband have retired and sold their shop and name to another framer.

I am not sure where Celia's drive to be the best that she could be for any undertaking came from. Perhaps it came as a competitive reaction to her older brother Saul's ability to excel in many areas.

Saul was intelligent enough to be accepted into Townsend Harris High School, which accepted only New York City's brightest students. He was also manually dexterous, able to build us a shed in our backyard to hold our garden tools. He built a rocking horse for our children, which was also passed on to our grandchildren. It now sits in our basement because it has outgrown its usefulness, but is too beautiful to throw away. Maybe it will be handed down to a great-grandchild.

Perhaps in having to compete for attention with her gifted sibling, Celia decided to do her best in any endeavor which she undertook. Take cooking. Celia not only cooked for her nuclear family, but she catered large dinner parties for holidays and special events like our sons' Bar Mitzvahs and weddings. Not only did she prepare delicious food, but she collected hundreds of cookbooks with which she expanded her recipes. Celia loved to prepare delectable food, but even more, she loved the compliments she received from her guests and the reputation she enjoyed for being known as a good cook. She never complained about the work involved in preparing food, but every once in a while, she tried to reckon how many meals she prepared in her lifetime. We were never able to reach even a ballpark estimate.

Celia's father, Nathan Grossman, was known for his keen sense of direction. When the Grossman family emigrated from Russia and landed in Canada, Nathan took a stroll down the strange streets of Montreal on the very first day and found his way back without the least bit of trouble. When the family finally moved to New York, Nathan could find any place in the city after being taken there just once. He seemed to have a global positioning system buried in his brain. This trait must have been passed on to his daughter, Celia, for she was an excellent navigator when we took various motor trips. When we were going camping with Lenore and Charley Becker at Emerald Lake State Park in Vermont, or visiting the Larkins when they moved to Massachusetts, or taking our sons to Howe Caverns in upstate New York, Celia found the way unerringly.

I, on the other hand, have almost no sense of direction. I once spent an hour driving around the Metropolitan Houses in the Bronx unable to find my way out of the apartment building complex because all the buildings and streets looked alike.

When we moved to our home in Little Neck, Queens, and I started to work as a teacher in East Harlem, Manhattan, it became evident that Celia would need to learn how to drive in order to do the shopping, run errands and, later on, drive to her own teaching job in Flushing. Fortunately we took the advice of friends who warned me not to try to teach my wife how to drive, but to let a professional instructor handle the job. One day the instructor from the American Automobile Club pulled up to our house in a car with dual controls and Celia was off on her first lesson. I don't know much about what went on during the lessons, but one time Celia told me what she had learned on that particular day. It had to do with using the signal lights when one wants to make a right or left turn. "Using your signal lights, just shows your intention to make a turn; it doesn't give you the right to make that turn," her instructor told her. His point, which Celia took to heart, was that the driver has to make sure it is safe to turn even after using the signal.

Celia did well during her lessons and she passed her driving test. However, she was comfortable driving only on local streets but not on the highways. Even though she restricted herself to local driving, Celia never got lost or had an accident while driving.

When Phil was about twelve years old and Steven was ten and a half, Celia decided to become a teacher. She went to Queens College and spoke with an advisor who noticed her background as a biology major and her work with the New York City Health Department.

"You could be a science teacher," the advisor said.

"I've been away from the field for a long time," Celia replied. "I don't think I want to teach science."

"Do you play the piano?" the advisor asked. She said she did. "Would you like to work with children in kindergarten?" She answered in the affirmative again and after that conversation Celia was on the road to her new career as a kindergarten teacher.

The registration process at Queens College at that time was chaotic and frustrating for the students. Celia failed to register on that first day and came home in tears. She went back on the next day and found a sympathetic advisor who helped her get through the registration process. Over several years Celia took her education courses and received her Master's degree and teaching certificate. Her teaching career lasted about 25 years, and she taught in the kindergarten class at the same school, P.S. 24, Queens. She enjoyed her work; the children and their parents liked her very much. Some parents along with students became personal friends and remained so long after the children were grown.

B.F. Skinner, the behavioral psychologist, wrote about his later life when his short-term memory was beginning to fail. To compensate for this condition, he developed a habit of writing things down, like the names of people whom he just met or a list of things he had to do for the day.

As a young woman Celia did not need to write things down because of a failing memory, but she did it anyway. Perhaps it was her training as a biologist working for the New York City Health Department. As part of her job she had to keep track of various tests she was running on the discharges of large companies. To do so she made a "To Do" list at the beginning of each workday.

When she retired from the Health Department to raise her family, she continued the practice of writing out her plans for the day on yellow, four-by-six-inch pads every day. She must have used up dozens of yellow pads as she made her plans and crossed off the items she accomplished each day.

This habit of Celia's proved helpful to our friends. While living in our new home on Thebes Avenue, we had become very close with our across-the-street neighbors, the Larkins. After many years together, almost like an extended family, the Larkins had to move to Massachusetts because Phil Larkin's employer wanted him to work out of their headquarters there. We were sad to see our good friends leave, but we promised to keep in touch and to visit whenever we could.

Late in the afternoon, on the day they left, we got a call from a distraught Phil Larkin. He told us that his wife, Margaret, was not handling the move well. She was unable to cope with the many piles of boxes which were placed willy-nilly in the various rooms of their new home. Knowing Celia's organizing skills, Phil asked us if we could come to help set up their new home. We said we would visit them on the weekend.

For the next two days, Celia and I, together with the Larkins, unpacked the boxes and set up the rooms, one at a time, until there was order where there had been chaos.

Celia, who had experience in setting up our apartment on East 65th Street and again in our new home in Queens, played a major role in helping the Larkins get their new home in order.

As a beginning teacher, starting in 1949, my salary was meager, not large enough to take a vacation during the summer months, except for one summer in 1951 when we took a cross-country trip with Laurie and Mimie Seidman all the way to California. Since we and the Seidmans had little money, we decided to save expenses by using campgrounds instead of motels when we stopped for the night. The trip itself was memorable, not only for the historic places we visited, the Badlands, Yosemite, the Grand Canyon, etc., but also for the fact that the old Oldsmobile, which we borrowed from Laurie's father, had four bald tires, which at various times blew out as we were traveling at sixty miles per hour. Once we ended up in a ditch on the side of the highway. A kind trucker came by, pulled our car out of the ditch with his truck and helped us change the tire. By the time we finished the trip to California, we had bought four new tires.

Later on, when our salaries increased, we were able to take longer trips and go across the country in a recreational vehicle (RV) which we shared with Celia's brother and sister-in-law, Saul and Roz. Unlike our previous trip with Laurie and Mimie, on this trip we were able to sleep in comfortable beds. Each night we would pull into a campground specifically designed for RV's with hook-ups for water, electricity and sewage. The first thing we would do after arriving at a campsite would be to hook up to these facilities.

I remember how surprised I was when Saul asked me to drive the large RV. Since the vehicle was equipped with automatic drive, I felt that it was not much different from driving an automobile.

During our trip, we stopped at familiar tourist attractions, such as the Corn Palace in Nebraska, the Badlands, the geysers, Mt. Rushmore with its four presidents carved in stone, the Grand Canyon and the neon-lit gambling casinos in Nevada.

I remember a stop we made at lunchtime near the Grand Canyon. We went into a luxurious restaurant which was built like a huge lodge. The four of us sat down and ordered from the menu, choosing a salad as our appetizer. When Saul stuck his fork into his salad, he uncovered a white paper towel, which was used to dry the freshly washed lettuce. However, instead of discarding the paper towel, the preparer left it in the salad and piled on more ingredients on top of it.

As Saul removed the paper towel, he held it up with his fork and asked, "Did everyone get one of these in the salad?" When the waitress and the Maitre D were summoned to our table and shown the errant paper towel, the waitress broke down in tears and the Maitre D ordered a fresh salad and put Saul's meal "on the house" as part of his apology. The incident reminded me of the following limerick:

> *There once was a man from Purdue*
> *Who found a large mouse in his stew.*
> *Said the waiter, "Don't shout and wave it about*
> *Or the rest will be wanting one, too!*

Another incident I remember as we traveled in our RV took place in Colorado, which is noted for its high altitude. It was our custom to stop around five o'clock in the evening and have some refreshments, including alcoholic drinks. When we reached Colorado we followed this ritual, unaware of the fact that high altitudes increase the potency of alcohol on the brain. We four were drinking gin and tonics and in a little while, we became drunk, feeling no pain and laughing for no reason at all. From that time on, when we stopped for drinks, I asked for "Tonic and tonic" instead of "Gin and tonic."

As a teacher I was able to enroll in a Health Maintenance Organization (HMO) called HIP for Health Insurance Program, which included coverage for the entire family. However, Celia availed herself of the doctors more than I did. After bearing two healthy boys, Phil and Steve, Celia developed cancer of the uterus and had a hysterectomy. She also suffered from glaucoma and later she developed cancer in her right breast and had a lumpectomy.

Celia never complained about her illnesses or asked, "Why me?" She just made her appointments, showed up on time and went through the various procedures as though they were routine.

One day on or about 1999, after she had retired from her job as a kindergarten teacher, she and I were in our family doctor's office for a routine check-up. Dr. Chasky noticed that Celia's face on the right side had a strange appearance. It seemed to be rigid and expressionless, as though she were wearing a mask on one side of her face. He asked Celia if she experienced difficulty in getting out of a chair. Celia acknowledged that she did. The doctor also noticed a slight tremor in her right hand. He told Celia that she might have Parkinson's disease, but he was not certain. Celia seemed to have the same symptoms that he had observed in his father-in-law, who was diagnosed as having the disease.

Dr. Chasky referred Celia to the neurologist on the staff, Dr. Haldea. The neurologist was a slightly built woman from India with gray hair. She examined Celia carefully. I was surprised to notice that the doctor used only motion exercises to confirm the diagnosis as Parkinson's disease. She asked Celia to put one hand on top of the other, one hand with the palm facing up and the covering hand with the palm down. Then she asked Celia to reverse the hands so that the opposite hands were palm up and palm down. Celia was asked to perform this maneuver rapidly several times. Then Dr. Haldea asked Celia to walk back and forth in the hallway near her office. With these simple tests, the dreadful diagnosis of Parkinson's disease was confirmed.

Dr. Haldea, whose waiting room was always full because she took so much time with her patients, talked with Celia and me for a long time, explaining that the disease had no known cure, but there were medications available that could relieve some of Celia's symptoms. She prescribed a dopamine-based pill that would help, once the correct dosage was determined.

The doctor asked Celia to return in three weeks in order to see if the medication was working. In fact, the medicine did have the desired effect on Celia's symptoms. Her right hand no longer had a tremor, and the right side of her face no longer had a mask-like appearance. Celia and I, as well as her doctors, were delighted with the reduction of her symptoms. We thought that since we noticed the symptoms of Parkinson's disease early in its onset, we would be ahead of the game, but that did not prove to be the case.

For several months, Celia was symptom-free, but then the effect of the medication seemed to wear off and her symptoms returned. Dr. Haldea prescribed higher doses of the medications and added an additional pill to relieve the symptoms, and that seemed to work for a few more months.

However, after a while the new dosages and the new medicine lost their effectiveness, we were losing the battle with Parkinson's in slow stages.

An MRI of Celia's brain revealed that her brain was deteriorating, either as a result of the disease or as a separate additional brain disorder. Her speech became slurred and then incomprehensible. At almost the same time she began to lose her ability to walk. Our medical group supplied her with a cane, then a walker, and finally a wheelchair.

Celia was now confined to sitting on a chair in the living room. When it was time to eat, I would help her to walk to the kitchen and reseat her onto a kitchen chair. All this sitting caused her to develop a bed sore on her rear end, which became worse over time. When I brought her to Dr. Chasky, he took one look at her wound and summoned the doctors of the wound center. They cleaned the wound and then made arrangements for the Visiting Nurse Service to have someone come to our house every day, including the weekend, to clean and dress the wound. Over time the wound improved, but it never healed completely because Celia was constantly sitting or lying on it.

Throughout all of these medical problems, Celia complained very little, but she became depressed. Dr. Haldea spent a great deal of time at the Jamaica HIP Center trying to deal with Celia's depression but to no avail. Celia's brain was shutting down little by little.

Among the casualties of this deterioration was her ability to read. One day as we were sitting in our living room, I noticed that during one hour Celia had not turned the page of the book she was reading. At times as we were sitting in our living room, Celia would say to me, "I want to go home." At first I took these words literally and told her that she was home. "This is your home," I would say. "This is where we live." My response never satisfied her. Later on or the next day she would ask again to be taken home. My response would be the same, but she would not accept it.

Slowly it dawned on me that her request to be taken home was metaphorical, not literal. "Home" was not a place but a "time" when her body and mind were functioning as they were meant to function. "I want to go home" meant "I want to be the way I used to be."

From then on I responded by holding her hand and telling her that I understood.

When Saul and Roz visited us and saw Celia's condition, Saul suggested that we get a stair-climber so that Celia could get upstairs to our bedroom on the second floor without having to struggle with the stairs. He also suggested that we get a home health aide for Celia so that the burden of care for Celia could be shared. Both of these suggestions made sense, so I called a chair lift company whose ad I had seen in *The New York Times*. After my phone call, two men came to our house and installed a chair lift in two hours. I then called the aide who had cared for my friend Laurie after his wife, Mimie, had died. The aide, Luisa, said that she had a job with another family so she was unavailable. However, she suggested another aide with whom she had worked when a patient needed around-the-clock care. The aide's name was Jean O'Neil and after a phone call, arrangements were made. Jeanie was a black woman from Jamaica with a slight build, black hair, and a melodious Jamaican accent.

She was very experienced in working with elderly infirm patients, and she was very gentle and caring with Celia. Jeanie was a great help to both Celia and me. She made our lunch and supper, helped when the visiting nurse came to change Celia's bandages on her buttocks and helped me get Celia to the doctor when we had an appointment. With Jeanie in the house, I could do the food shopping and not have to worry about Celia. When Jeanie was not busy tending to Celia, she cleaned the house from top to bottom. She scrubbed our carpets and washed our curtains.

After Jeanie came to work for us, our lives settled into a routine. Jeanie arrived from her home in Brooklyn about nine o'clock in the morning. By that time I had awakened Celia, washed and dressed her, combed her hair and given her breakfast. After breakfast Jeanie would give Celia a shower upstairs using a special chair which was kept in the bathroom for that purpose, and then return her to her chair in the living room. Around ten or eleven o'clock in the morning, a nurse from the Visiting Nurse Service would arrive to clean Celia's wound and put on fresh bandages. This involved moving Celia from her chair in the living room to her hospital bed set up in the back of our house, an extension that we had built many years ago and referred to as "the den." When Celia was able to walk a little, I helped her walk the distance from the living room to the den. If she was unable to walk, Jeanie and I moved Celia onto a wheelchair and moved her into the den.

Jeanie and I would help the visiting nurse as she removed the old bandage from Celia's wound and washed it with distilled water. Then the nurse would put on sterile rubber gloves and apply Polysporin powder to the wound and put on a fresh bandage.

We had several appointments at the HIP wound center where a team of specialists would examine Celia's wound, measure it and prescribe new medication. After the visiting nurse left, Celia would remain in bed and rest while Jeanie would prepare lunch for the three of us.

Sometimes after lunch Jeanie would take Celia for a walk in the wheelchair. She would walk up and down the block just to get Celia out of the house and get some fresh air.

Around 4:30 in the afternoon, Jeanie would prepare our supper. Sometimes we would have spaghetti and tomato sauce and sometimes I would prepare a dish of rice and fried vegetables. Jeanie liked to spice up the dish with Tabasco sauce. Then after supper

Jeanie would help me to put Celia to bed. We put Celia in the stair climber which brought her up to the second floor where our bedroom was located. We got her undressed, into her nightgown and put her to bed. It seemed strange to go to bed so early when it was still light out, and it reminded me of my childhood when I was put to bed at about the same time.

Celia proved to be a good sleeper. As soon as her head hit the pillows, she fell asleep and did not wake up until morning. While Celia was sleeping, I got into bed and watched the news on our TV. The sound didn't seem to bother Celia, so I watched my favorite programs and went to bed after Johnny Carson's monologue.

In the morning I washed and dressed and then woke up Celia. I washed and dressed her, combed her hair and prepared breakfast for the two of us. At nine a.m. Jeanie would arrive and would take care of Celia.

After a while our days settled into a routine which were more or less predictable. However, there were times when Celia had an appointment with her primary care physician, the wound care team, her neurologist, or her eye doctor. For these appointments Jeanie and I would get Celia in her wheelchair, transport her to the car, fold up the wheelchair and store it in the trunk. Upon reaching the HIP center, we would repeat the process. Throughout this process of getting in and out of her wheelchair, Celia never complained even though it was difficult for her to move around.

She endured examinations like X-rays, and MRI's with stoic patience. As time went on, I began to feel that Celia's Parkinson's disease had stabilized. It was not improving, but it was manageable.

But then, at times, I would notice that Celia kept her eyes closed even after she was awake, washed and dressed. Thinking that this was some willful action on her part, I kept urging her to open her eyes but to no avail. When I mentioned this to her ophthalmologist, Dr. Fox, he informed me that the closing of the eyes was a common problem among patients with Parkinson's disease. He injected some Botox above Celia's eyebrows, and sure enough the problem vanished, at least for a while. After several weeks, the Botox lost its effect, and she had to have another injection.

As time wore on, Celia's ability to function as a human being began to wane. She was unable to speak, read, or walk. Her primary physician said that her brain was deteriorating, whether as a result of Parkinson's or some other cause was not clear.

Mercifully, on the night of June 12, 2002, Celia died in her sleep. When I tried to wake her in the morning, I found her unresponsive. Her skin was cool to my touch. I. dialed 911, and while I waited for the ambulance, I administered CPR with the guidance of the technician who stayed on the line.

I had taken a CPR course many years before this, but I never thought I would have to use the procedure on my wife. However, I was unable to restart Celia's heart beat and breathing. The emergency technicians who arrived several minutes after my phone call were also unable to revive Celia. While they were working on Celia in our upstairs bedroom, two police officers took me downstairs to our living room where they asked me for information about Celia's illness, date of birth, doctor's name and so forth.

The officers called my son, Phil, who soon came to our home from Long Beach. They also called Dr. Chasky, who verified that Celia was under his care and said he would sign the death certificate.

Steve also arrived and together we went to the funeral home to make arrangements. We used the same funeral home, Sinai Chapel, that we had used for Celia's mother, Sarah, and my father, Herman.

With the help of Phil and Steve we contacted relatives and friends and told them about Celia's death. Those who could came to the funeral and burial at the new Montefiore Cemetery where Celia and her family had grave sites.

CHAPTER THIRTY-ONE
Life after Celia

I USED TO THINK THAT MOST religious practices or rites were illogical remnants from the past. However, after I almost recovered from the shock of Celia's death and the realization that my life-long partner was gone and would never return, I began to appreciate the value of the rites surrounding the death of a loved one. First of all, the rites "tell you what to do." For example, in most religions, funeral arrangements of some kind have to be made. This involves notifying family and friends of the death and the funeral information. In the Catholic religion there is the wake before the funeral where relatives and friends gather to say goodbye to the deceased and to comfort the mourners with their presence. The Jewish rites do not have a wake, but relatives and friends gather at the chapel to comfort one another before the formal funeral service consisting of prayers and eulogies.

After the burial at the cemetery, religious Jews have a period of mourning lasting about a week where the mourner *sits shiva* which is somewhat analogous to the wake whereby friends and family visit the mourner to convey their condolences. While these practices appear to be ritualistic, they have a psychological purpose: to surround the mourners with friends and family so that the bereaved do not feel alone or abandoned.

At first friends and relatives visited me even after the week of *sitting shiva.* In a way it was comforting to talk to my visitors about the good times Celia and I had together. After a week or two the visits became less frequent, and I was left to deal with my loss by myself. It was at that time that the realization that my life's partner was gone forever and that I would have to carry on somehow without my Celia. In a deep depression, I kept thinking of the phrase, "Stop the world, I want to get off." I asked our home aide,

Jeanie, to stay on for a few weeks to help clear away Celia's clothes and belongings. For the most part I just sat in the living room and tried to get through each day. I got up each morning and prepared my breakfast.

Jeanie prepared lunch for the two of us, and when she left around 4:30 in the afternoon, I started to prepare my supper. As I was preparing my lonely meal, I was made aware of the fact that every single item in the kitchen was brought and used by Celia. As I cut salad vegetables. I used the little black paring knife that was Celia's favorite. When I stirred up eggs and milk for scrambled eggs, I used the same fork that she had used for so many years. In fact, almost everything in our house was made or bought by Celia and every time I used an implement or looked at a framed picture I thought of her.

A year passed and I realized that I couldn't spend all my time sitting around and doing nothing useful. I decided to ask for my old job back at the college in Westchester where I had been a professional tutor in the writing program for eighteen years. I wanted something useful to do. I had only worked two days a week from eight to three, not a difficult stint by any means. More importantly, I had enjoyed the work which was to go over students' writing in a one-on-one session. I would make suggestions on how to improve the organization of the paper and how to correct errors in grammar or usage. Usually the student felt better about her writing after she left the session. I also went into classrooms and made short presentations on grammar skills. One teacher called me "The Grammar Guy." When I called the director, and told him I would like to return, he welcomed me back with enthusiasm.

My next call was to my friend, Estelle Cohen (no relation) who used to order theater tickets for Celia and me for shows that were presented at Queens Community College. The shows, consisting of dancers, singers, and comedians were entertaining, and the prices were reasonable. Since the college was only ten minutes away from our house, the theater was easy to get to, and there was plenty of parking. Celia and I and Estelle and her friend, Walter, had attended these shows for many years, so I was eager to re-subscribe. Estelle kindly agreed to handle my subscription. Little did I know that I was to receive more than theater tickets with that one phone call.

Chapter Thirty-Two

A new friend

WHEN I ARRIVED AT THE Queens Community College theater, Estelle greeted me and introduced me to her friend, Gladys Barkas, who lived two houses away from Estelle. Gladys had asked Estelle to buy tickets for several shows at the College, just as I had. As we sat down next to each other waiting for the show to begin, Gladys and I began to become acquainted. "Guess how old I am?" she asked me.

"Sixty-five," I answered, trying to play it safe.

"Well, I'm eighty-two."

"You don't look anywhere near eighty-two."

"Well, I am, and I'm wearing a wig."

Glady, as she liked to be called, wore a blond curly wig. She had a light, small frame of a body and large brown eyes. She told me about herself, and asked me about my life. During the course of our conversation, Glady informed me that she had been a kindergarten teacher, that one of her former students was to be married in January, and that she had been invited to his wedding. Glady also informed me that the formal invitation was for "Gladys Barkas and guest." I thought to myself that surely a beautiful woman like Glady would have no trouble finding an escort for the wedding and that she was just making conversation when she told me about the wedding invitation.

Since we had tickets for six or seven shows that season, Glady and I met several times over the next few months. It was in December, around Chanukah, when I received a card from Glady wishing me a happy holiday. Slowly it dawned on me that Glady was sending me signals, but I was too dense to notice them. Maybe the Chanukah card meant that she liked me, and maybe the previous conversation about the wedding invitation, including a guest, was a signal that she wanted me to be her escort to that affair in January.

I telephoned Glady and asked her if I could be her guest for the wedding, and she said, "I would be delighted to have you as my escort."

This proved the beginning of a friendship which has lasted for four years and is still going strong.

We did go to the wedding between Michael Koch and Paula. We danced and ate and had a great time together. People kept asking us how long we have been married because, I suppose, we looked like we had known each other a long time. As the wedding progressed, I thought that Glady must have been a great kindergarten teacher if her pupil remembered her for all those years and invited her to his wedding so many years later.

In recounting her history to me, Glady told me a story about her younger days before she was married when she would go on dates with would-be suitors. At the end of the date she would inform her escorts that she did not kiss on the first date. I took this revelation as a signal that I should not try to kiss Glady on the lips until after our second date.

The trouble was we did not have a second date. Rather, we just hung out together. Since neither of us liked to have dinner alone, we arranged to have dinner together at Glady's house in Bayside, which was only eight minutes away by car from my house in Little Neck. Our dinners were simple, consisting of New England clam chowder, which was Glady's favorite soup, spaghetti with tomato sauce, salads, and shrimp with cocktail sauce. The shrimp came from a fish stall in a market on 73rd Avenue. They were large shrimp, neatly shelled and veined. We also made hamburgers and hot dogs. Glady's favorite vegetables were broccoli and creamed spinach which came in a frozen package.

Glady's daughter, Jan, observed that we were "playing house." However, we did not consider these cooking sessions as "dates," so I refrained from trying to kiss Glady on the lips, confining myself to a harmless peck on her cheek.

During our many conversations, I mentioned that my family

did not care much for birthday celebrations. I could not remember a time when my grandmother, grandfather or any other of my numerous aunts and uncles ever had a birthday party with the traditional cake and candles. My Aunt Mamie and Aunt Ray were the only ones, except for my Dad, who acknowledged my birthday by giving me a present, usually an item of clothing like a shirt or a tie. My Dad once bought me a scooter for one of my birthdays which I rode till it fell apart.

Upon hearing this, Glady made up her mind to arrange a huge party for my 81st birthday. It turned out to be a very happy occasion with about fifty guests. It was a catered affair held in Glady's family room, which was a spacious extension built onto her original house.

Although our formal invitations requested that no presents were necessary, because I did not need any more "stuff," many guests ignored the message and brought me presents, more than I had ever received during my childhood years. Aside from the delicious food and birthday cake, one of the best parts of the party was the way our two families, Glady's and mine, came together and became friends. I will never again mention to anyone that I had been neglected in the birthday celebration department.

Finally, during the birthday party which Glady had arranged for me, I declared that the carefully planned party could be considered a second date so I kissed her on the lips in front of all the invited guests. At this point Peggy, Glady's younger sister, exclaimed, "What took you so long. You're not getting any younger, you know."

This is how Glady and I formed a warm, lasting relationship and I can kiss her on the lips whenever I want to.

EPILOGUE

If

AS A RULE, I AM A QUIET PERSON in terms of making conversation. I tend to keep my thoughts bottled up. Glady, however, will tell you her life story at the drop of a hat, and what is more, she has the unique ability to get people, even perfect strangers, to open up and reveal themselves. So in our many conversations, I played the part of a bottle sealed with a tight cap and Glady played the part of a lady with a bottle opener. That is to say she prodded me to tell her my life's history. Once I did, she suggested I write a book. And so with Glady's enthusiastic encouragement, I began to write the book you are now reading.

One day on a Saturday afternoon, as we were attending our weekly session of the short story club, Glady, with her metaphorical bottle opener in hand, announced to the club members that "Larry is writing his autobiography." After digesting this news from out of the blue, some members, including Chris, the group leader, asked if they could read some of my work along with the short stories they were reading each week. Although I would never have revealed my writing project to any one, for my intention was to complete the autobiography, get it published somehow, and send a copy to my family and friends, I soon realized that the opportunity to present my writing, a few pages at a time, to a group of avid readers, would be invaluable for the same reason that a stage play is often tried out in Philadelphia before it opens on Broadway.

Along with authors like Henry James, Edgar Allan Poe, Doris Lessing, and Dorothy Parker, our reading group was also reading Larry Cohen, who was delighted to be in such illustrious company.

All of the above is meant to say that without Gladys Barkas and her enthusiastic support, this book in all probability would never have been written, or it would have existed only in my head and not on paper.

I believe that important highlights of my life have come about because of what grammarians call "dependent clauses" beginning with the word "*if*."

For example, *if* Glady and I had not asked our mutual friend Estelle Cohen to order tickets for us for those shows at Queensboro Community College, then Glady and I would never have met.

If Glady had not been invited to the Koch wedding because she was such a gifted kindergarten teacher for the groom, Glady and I would never have had our first date and subsequent close relationship.

Similarly, *if* my wife Celia and I had not lived in the same upper Westside Manhattan neighborhood, and *if* we had not been assigned to Monsieur Perry's French class, we may never have met, married, and been husband and wife for 55 years.

If a German soldier had aimed his burp gun slightly higher when he grazed my left knee and punctured a toe on my left foot, my life story would have been much shorter.

If in Camp Shelby, Mississippi, where I contracted a severe case of spinal meningitis, if the doctors had not had sulfanilamide drugs to fight the disease, I would have become a casualty of war.

And finally, *if* my mother had not been stricken with post partum depression, for which the doctors had no medication, my family may not have broken apart and scattered and I would not have been *almost an orphan.*

THE END

About The Author

LAWRENCE H. COHEN (or Larry, as his friends and colleagues know him) was born in Uniontown, Pennsylvania and grew up in the Bronx and the Fort Washington section of Manhattan in the 1920's and 1930's. He served in the U.S. Army during World War II and returned from service to receive his undergraduate degree from the City College of New York (CCNY) on the G.I. Bill. He went on to obtain his a doctorate in education from Teachers College of Columbia University. Dr. Cohen is retired from a thirty-year career in elementary education as a classroom teacher, reading specialist, and supervisor. At present, he works as a teacher and professional tutor in the writing program at a college in Westchester County, New York. Married to his wife Celia for 55 years before she died in 2002, he is the father of two grown sons and five grandchildren. He lives in Little Neck, New York.

www.ingramcontent.com/pod-product-compliance
Lightning Source LLC
Chambersburg PA
CBHW031256090426
42742CB00007B/486